way up north
WISCONSIN
COOKBOOK

Recipes and Foodways from God's Country

VICTORIA SHEARER

Globe
Pequot

ESSEX, CONNECTICUT

Globe Pequot

An imprint of Globe Pequot, the trade division of
The Rowman & Littlefield Publishing Group, Inc.
4501 Forbes Blvd., Ste. 200
Lanham, MD 20706
www.rowman.com

Distributed by NATIONAL BOOK NETWORK

British Library Cataloguing in Publication Information available

Library of Congress Cataloging-in-Publication Data

Names: Shearer, Victoria, author.
Title: Way up north Wisconsin cookbook : recipes and foodways from God's
    Country / Victoria Shearer.
Description: Essex, Connecticut : Globe Pequot, [2024] | Includes index. |
    Summary: "Once a remote primeval forest settled by iron and copper miners
    and then lumberjacks, Up North Wisconsin is now an extremely popular
    vacation destination, drawing vacationers from Illinois, Iowa, Minnesota,
    Michigan, and parts beyond, year 'round, who enjoy its 3,200 lakes, streams,
    and a half million acres of public forest. More than just a cookbook, *Way Up
    North Wisconsin Cookbook* celebrates the history, the people, and cultures
    that so influenced the area for centuries with a compilation of recipes
    presenting a fresh take on traditional foods alongside interesting sidebars on
    the quintessential uniqueness that makes Up North Wisconsin"— Provided by
    publisher.
Identifiers: LCCN 2023037586 (print) | LCCN 2023037587 (ebook) | ISBN
    9781493070848 (trade paperback) | ISBN 9781493070855 (epub)
Subjects: LCSH: Cooking, American—Midwestern style. | Cooking—Wisconsin.
    | LCGFT: Cookbooks.
Classification: LCC TX715.2.M53 S54 2024 (print) | LCC TX715.2.M53 (ebook) |
    DDC 641.59775—dc23/eng/20230912
LC record available at https://lccn.loc.gov/2023037586
LC ebook record available at https://lccn.loc.gov/2023037587

Printed in India

Contents

The Way Up North Experience, v

The Starting Lineup, 1

Soup's On!, 25

Out of Hand, 43

Oodles of Noodles, 59

Savory Pies, 77

The Main Events, 89

Farmers' Market, 133

Side Shows, 155

Sweet Finales, 173

Breakfast All Day, 199

Index, 217

Acknowledgments, 219

About the Author, 220

Sand Lake is tucked away nine miles deep in the woods from Mercer. VICTORIA SHEARER

The Way Up North Experience

WISCONSIN BORN AND BRED, I've been coming "Up North" since I was a little girl—Way Up North. My dad always called it "God's Country." A thinly populated region of more than a million acres of public forests and more than half of Wisconsin's 15,000 lakes, rivers, and streams, Up North reigns supreme as a pristine natural escape, a throwback to yesteryear's simpler times.

Where Up North begins has always been up for debate. Most would agree, though, any area north of Highway 8 is definitely Way Up North. For me, it was always when the farmland stopped and thick forests blanketed the horizon and a peppering of lakes came into view. Wherever one thinks Up North begins, most everyone agrees that you know it when you get there.

My family's special place was Sand Lake, a tiny "pot" lake deep in the woods, nine miles from Mercer. Northern Wisconsin was heavily glaciated in the Pleistocene era. When the ice began to melt about 20,000 years ago, the water melted unevenly over the next several hundred years, eventually resting in irregular-shaped "potholes," and thus forming the thousands of deep, spring-fed lakes in the area, known as "kettle lakes" or "pot lakes."

My parents found their little piece of God's Country on their honeymoon and built a one-room cabin in 1949. Ours is a common tale in these parts: originally no electricity, no running water, a potbellied stove, an icebox, an outhouse out back. Over the years, one room led to two, two to three, three to four, then, one by one, amenities became available, and cabins were modernized. Just like mine, many cabins Up North have been passed down, generation to generation.

Our cabin, the Loon's Nest, present day. VICTORIA SHEARER

Life is different up here. Casual. Laid-back. Sporty. Uncomplicated. Like our lifestyle, our food culture is simple and hearty, a rich tapestry derived from the influence of immigrant settlements more than a century ago. Whereas German settlements made an impact on the cultural life of southern Wisconsin (think sausage, cheese, and beer), Swedes, Norwegians, and Finns settled in northern Wisconsin, where they worked in the lumber camps and mines that were booming in the late 1800s and early 1900s and added their own culinary cultures to the mix. (The Finns are also credited with introducing notched log cabins, an architectural style still very common in the Northwoods today.)

People come Up North seeking quiet, space, sparkling lakes, and forests teeming with wildlife. The wind through the pines, the call of the loons, the sighting of a white-tailed deer or a sandhill crane—there's a continuity to life in the Northwoods. Nothing much seems to change. Family and friends gather every summer. Generations of kids have jumped off docks into cold, clear water; pedal-boated through water lily gardens; gone water-skiing and tubing.

You can't beat a day on or in the water. VICTORIA SHEARER

Pattison State Park's Big Manitou Falls roaringly cascades 165 feet down a deep-sided gorge. SHUTTERSTOCK

The shores of Lake Superior are a great place to kayak.
BAYFIELD CHAMBER OF COMMERCE

We hike miles of scenic trails, float down rivers and streams, canoe and kayak, and visit our plethora of majestic waterfalls and the spectacular Lake Superior.

And, of course, we fish . . . and fish . . . and fish. Fishing our prolific waters for walleye, bass, trout, and panfish leads to tall fish tales and great fry-ups. Hooking the sport fish muskellunge (Wisconsin's state fish; also known as the "muskie") is considered quite an accomplishment. (There are 200 muskie lakes within a nine-mile radius of Boulder Junction, dubbed the Muskie Capital of the World, and a four-story concrete muskie fronts the National Freshwater Fishing Hall of Fame in Hayward.)

Generations of men have dropped everything, hitting the woods the minute deer-hunting season starts in the fall. And scores of off-roaders race ATVs and "side-by-sides" along the hundreds of miles of groomed trails through our forests

My gang is always ready to drop a line. VICTORIA SHEARER

My father (left) hunting with family and friends at our original cabin, circa 1950s.
VICTORIA SHEARER

Off-roaders enjoying the groomed trails snaking through our woods.
SHUTTERSTOCK

This is our "special place that brings peace of mind." VICTORIA SHEARER

in the summer and autumn, replaced in the dead of winter by snowmobilers who descend on the snow-covered Northwoods trails.

So, what is Way Up North exactly? Some people think it's simply a state of mind, but I think Susan Kindler captures it best in this 1996 poem:

> It's the place people go to escape,
> a place made of cabins, pine trees and lakes.
> But no matter how far you drive,
> There's no sign to say "You've arrived."
> So just follow your heart 'til you find,
> Your special place that brings peace of mind.
> As you breathe in the air and unwind,
> Your cares are all left behind.
> It's no mystery where the Northwoods start.
> When you're "up north," you'll know in your heart.

The lower portion of Lost Creek Falls in Cornucopia exudes an almost mystical ambience. BAYFIELD CHAMBER OF COMMERCE

The Starting Lineup

Apricot Baked Brie

French cheese producers make much of their Brie cheese in Wisconsin because the composition of Wisconsin's milk closely resembles that found in France. The application of Penicillium candidum, *the white mold you see on the surface of Brie, produces enzymes that ripen the cheese from the outside in.*

1 (16-ounce) wheel Brie cheese

⅔ cup apricot preserves, divided

2 tablespoons finely minced jalapeño peppers, divided

½ cup finely chopped pecans, divided

1 "you bake it" baguette

Cut Brie in half horizontally, through the center of the wheel of cheese. Place bottom half of Brie wheel (cut-side up) in the center of a large, shallow, round baking dish. Spread ⅓ cup preserves atop cheese. Sprinkle with 1 tablespoon jalapeños and ¼ cup pecans. Place other half of Brie atop preserves, cut-side down. Spread remaining preserves atop Brie. Sprinkle with remaining tablespoon peppers and ¼ cup pecans.

Preheat the oven to 350 degrees F. Cut baguette into ¼-inch slices. Place baguette slices on a baking sheet on an upper rack in the oven. Place Brie on the lower oven rack and bake both Brie and bread for 10 minutes. Place toasted bread surrounding Brie in the baking dish. Serve immediately.

(SERVES 16 TO 20)

Baked Nachos

Colby cheese was first made by Wisconsin cheesemakers in the late 1800s. It is a milder form of cheddar. Monterey Jack is a mild-flavored, semi-hard cheese that has a high fat and moisture content, which allows it to melt smoothly.

1 cup refried pinto beans

1 (10.75-ounce) can cheddar cheese soup

½ (13-ounce) bag restaurant-style white tortilla chips

1 (2.25-ounce) can sliced black olives, drained

1 cup chopped sweet onions, like Vidalia

1 cup diced tomatoes

¼ cup minced jalapeño peppers

4 ounces shredded Colby cheese

4 ounces shredded Monterey Jack cheese

Sour cream, for serving (optional)

Salsa, for serving (optional)

Guacamole, for serving (optional)

Preheat oven to 400 degrees F. Place refried beans and cheese soup in a medium-size microwave-safe bowl and stir to combine. Microwave for 1½ minutes.

Meanwhile, place tortilla chips in a single, even layer on a large baking sheet. Place more chips strategically over any spaces between chips. Pour cheese sauce over chips. Sprinkle olives, onions, tomatoes, and jalapeños atop cheese-sauce layer. Top with shredded Colby and Monterey Jack cheeses. Bake nachos for 5 minutes or until cheese has melted. Serve with sour cream, salsa, and guacamole, if desired.

(SERVES 8)

Brown Sugar Beer Sausage

Smoked sausage is fully cooked and cured, with an edible casing. The slow cooking in this recipe permeates the sausage with the flavors of the brown sugar and beer. Serve a wedge of Wisconsin Gouda alongside this easy, tasty appetizer for a showing of the famous Wisconsin triumvirate—beer, sausage, and cheese!

2 cups brown sugar

1 (12-ounce) can lager beer

1 pound smoked sausage, cut into ½-inch-thick slices

1 tablespoon cornstarch

Early in the day or one day ahead: Place brown sugar and beer in a 1½-quart slow cooker. Whisk until sugar has dissolved. Add sausage slices. Stir to combine. Cover slow cooker and cook on low for 5 hours. Transfer sausages and liquid to a covered container and refrigerate for several hours or overnight, until grease congeals on the top.

To serve: Skim off grease with a spoon and discard. Remove sausages with a slotted spoon and place in a medium bowl, reserving the liquid. In a small bowl, whisk together cornstarch and 2 tablespoons of liquid, forming a smooth paste. Transfer remaining reserved liquid to a medium nonstick saucepan over medium heat. Whisk in cornstarch mixture. Bring to a boil, stirring occasionally. Reduce heat to medium-low and cook for 10 minutes, stirring frequently. (Liquid will thicken and caramelize.) Add sausages and simmer until they are heated through, about 3 minutes. Transfer sausages and sauce to a 1½-quart slow cooker and hold on warm for up to 3 hours. To serve, place a fondue fork next to the slow cooker so guests can spear the sausages. (Guests should re-cover slow cooker between servings.)

(SERVES 6 TO 8)

Cocktail Skewers

Two of Italy's favorite starters appear together in a star appearance on these skewers. Taste the ingredients on one end and you'll enjoy a bite of prosciutto and melon. Eat the offerings on other end and you'll savor a tiny caprese salad—mozzarella, basil, and tomato. Wisconsin cheesemaker Crave Brothers makes their cherry-sized mozzarella ciliegini from milk that comes from cows that graze right across the road from their facility.

25 to 30 (4-inch) wooden skewers

½ cantaloupe, seeded and scooped with a melon baller

1 (3-ounce) package thinly sliced prosciutto, cut into ½-inch strips

1 (8-ounce) container (about 25) miniature mozzarella balls (*ciliegini*)

3 large fresh basil leaves, cut into 1-inch strips and strips cut in half

25 to 30 small grape tomatoes

Salt and freshly ground black pepper

Aged balsamic vinegar (optional)

Early in the day: Assemble ingredients on cocktail skewers. Skewer 1 melon ball. Fold up 1 strip of prosciutto and thread it onto the skewer. Add 1 mozzarella ball to the skewer, then a basil piece, and finally a grape tomato. Place in a large, covered container. Repeat with remaining skewers until all ingredients are used. Cover container and refrigerate until needed.

To serve: Place skewers on a serving plate. Season with salt and pepper to taste. Add a fine drizzle of balsamic vinegar, if desired. Serve at room temperature.

(MAKES 25 TO 30)

Of Course We Curd

In Wisconsin, Little Miss Muffet sat on her tuffet eating ... fried cheese curds! No whey, we say!

What the cheesesteak is to Philadelphia, fried cheese curds are to the dairy state. A unique Wisconsin delicacy, they are essentially unaged cheese that has been separated from the whey early in the cheese-making process. Bacterial cultures and the enzyme rennet are added to the milk, which is heated. About halfway through the process, the heated milk curdles, separating into solids and liquid—the curds and the whey.

Most of the curds get pressed into molds and aged to form what we see as the blocks of cheese we see at the supermarket. The remaining irregularly shaped curds are salted and sold fresh as a "squeaky" snack food. (The squeak you may hear when you bite into the curd is an indication of its freshness and is caused by the elastic protein strands inside the cheese rubbing against your teeth. As cheese ages, the strands break down, and the squeak fades away.)

Fresh cheese curds are a great high-protein snack on their own, right out of the bag, but perhaps the most popular way to consume them are beer-battered and deep-fried—warm, light, and gooey. You'll find the tasty morsels offered on almost every Up North menu. Or order cheese curds online like I did at pasturepridecheese.com and try this easy recipe.

Fried Cheese Curds

6 cups (48 ounces) canola oil

1 cup flour

1 teaspoon baking powder

1 teaspoon salt

1 large egg, beaten

1 cup lager beer

1 (12-ounce) package Muenster cheese curds

In a deep fryer, heat oil to 375 degrees F. In a medium bowl, combine flour, baking powder, and salt. Whisk in beaten egg and beer until smooth. Working in batches of about 6 curds at a time, place curds in beer batter and stir to coat them thoroughly. Remove curds from batter with a slotted spoon, shaking off any excess. Place battered curds in the fryer basket, careful that they are not touching each other, and lower them into the oil following manufacturer's instructions. Fry curds for 45 seconds to 1 minute. Remove fried curds and drain them on paper toweling. Repeat process, working in batches, with remaining cheese curds. Serve immediately.

(SERVES 4)

Faux Seafood Biscuit Baskets

Imitation crab and imitation lobster are actually processed products made from a white fish called pollock. Less than two percent of the product is actually crab or lobster, but the fish is flavored to taste like the real deal and is much less expensive.

1 (8-ounce) package imitation crab meat, finely chopped

1 (8-ounce) package imitation lobster meat, finely chopped

1 (1.6-ounce) package dry Knorr Alfredo mix

1½ cups milk

1 tablespoon butter

1 teaspoon snipped fresh chives

2 (12-ounce) packages Pillsbury Grands Junior flaky biscuits

8 ounces fresh mozzarella cheese, finely shredded

Up to 1 month ahead: Preheat oven to 375 degrees F. Mix imitation crab and lobster meats together in a large bowl. In a medium saucepan over medium heat, whisk together Alfredo mix and milk. Add butter and bring mixture to a boil, whisking frequently. Reduce heat to low and cook 2 minutes more, whisking constantly. Whisk in chives. Pour Alfredo sauce over seafood mixture and stir until ingredients are well combined.

Coat a 24-count mini-muffin pan with vegetable cooking spray. Working with several biscuits at a time, and keeping the rest refrigerated, divide each biscuit into 3 flat pieces of dough. Stretch dough into a circle. Press each circle of dough into a muffin cup, forming a dough basket. Place a kitchen teaspoonful of seafood mixture into each dough basket. (Basket should be about three-quarters full.) Top with a generous sprinkling of cheese.

Bake for 11 to 12 minutes, until biscuit baskets are lightly browned and cheese is bubbly. Remove from oven and allow them to cool for 5 minutes. Gently transfer biscuit baskets to a wire rack and cool completely. Place in a covered container and refrigerate or freeze until needed. Repeat with remaining seafood filling and biscuits.

To reheat: Preheat oven to 325 degrees F. Place desired number of biscuit baskets on a baking sheet. Bake for 10 minutes, until biscuit baskets have heated through. Serve immediately.

(MAKES 54 APPETIZERS)

Mushroom Pastry Pinwheels

Puff pastry is a light, flaky pastry made from dozens of thin layers of buttery dough. Made from scratch, it is a laborious task at best. But luckily, puff pastry can be found, ready to bake, in the freezer section of most supermarkets and is incredibly easy to work with, with spectacular results.

1 (17.3-ounce) package puff pastry (2 sheets)

5 tablespoons butter

1½ cups chopped sweet onions, like Vidalia

1 pound baby bella or button mushrooms, finely chopped

1 teaspoon fresh lemon juice

1 tablespoon fruit-flavored honey mustard

⅛ teaspoon Worcestershire sauce

Pinch coarse salt

Freshly ground black pepper

2 tablespoons flour

Swiss cheese, for serving (optional)

Up to 1 month ahead: Place puff pastry at room temperature to defrost. Melt butter in a large nonstick skillet over medium heat. Add onions and mushrooms and sauté, stirring frequently, until all liquid has evaporated, about 8 minutes. Stir in lemon juice, mustard, Worcestershire sauce, salt, and pepper to taste. Sprinkle flour over mushroom mixture and cook for 2 minutes more, stirring frequently. Place skillet on a hot pad in the refrigerator to allow mushroom mixture to rapidly cool.

Unroll puff pastry sheets and even out the rectangles with a rolling pin. Spread half of the cooled mushroom mixture evenly atop each puff pastry sheet. Starting at the short side of each sheet, roll pastry over mushroom mixture, forming a long log. Press pastry at seam to seal. Roll each log into a sheet of cling wrap then cover with aluminum foil. Freeze until needed.

Up to 2 hours ahead: Unwrap mushroom logs and place them on a cutting board to defrost for 15 to 20 minutes. Preheat oven to 350 degrees F. Slice each semi-defrosted mushroom log into ½-inch slices with a serrated knife. Place slices, mushroom-side down, 2 inches apart on a parchment-paper-lined baking sheet. Bake for 25 to 30 minutes, until golden. Keep at room temperature until serving. Serve as a cracker-type snack or topped with thinly sliced Swiss cheese.

(MAKES 5 DOZEN APPETIZERS)

Beer Cheese Dips

Add Wisconsin cheese to Wisconsin beer and you, too, can become a "cheesehead!"

Cold Beer Cheese Dip

1 (8-ounce) carton whipped cream cheese

½ cup lager beer

1 cup Dutch Gouda cheese, finely shredded on a zester

1¼ teaspoons dry Hidden Valley Ranch dip mix

Wheat Thins crackers or Pretzel Crisps, for serving

At least 1 hour ahead: In a medium bowl, whisk together cream cheese and beer. Add finely shredded cheese and dip mix. Whisk until smooth. Refrigerate until needed. Serve with Wheat Thins crackers or Pretzel Crisps for dipping.

(SERVES 4 TO 6)

Warm Beer Cheese Dip

1 (6-count) package frozen soft pretzels, like Super Pretzel brand

1 tablespoon butter

1½ teaspoons garlic paste or finely minced garlic

1 tablespoon flour

¾ cup lager beer, like Leinenkugal

1½ teaspoons honey Dijon mustard

½ teaspoon Hungarian paprika

3 ounces whipped cream cheese

2 strips bacon, diced, fried until crispy, and drained

1 cup shredded sharp cheddar cheese

1 cup shredded Gruyère cheese

Preheat oven and bake soft pretzels according to package directions.

While pretzels are cooking, melt butter in a medium saucepan over medium heat. Add garlic and cook for 1 minute. Stir in flour and cook for 1 minute. Reduce heat to medium-low and slowly stir in beer, mustard, paprika, cream cheese, and bacon. Simmer until creamy. Reduce heat to low and stir in cheddar and Gruyère cheeses, stirring constantly until cheeses have melted and mixture is smooth and creamy. Transfer to a serving bowl and serve with warm soft pretzels.

(SERVES 4 TO 6)

Warm or cold, beer cheese dip is an Up North favorite. DAIRY FARMERS OF WISCONSIN

Northwoods Marys

Up North we take our Bloody Marys seriously—*very* seriously. Everyone knows what a Bloody Mary cocktail is, but few have experienced the lengths Up North Wisconsinites will go with its creation. First of all, the drink is served with a beer chaser, called a "snit." But perhaps more importantly, the Mary is served with competitively over-the-top garnishes that spill over the glass, often a meal in itself.

Our Marys' garnishes start where other states' end, with a pickle, a couple of olives, and a stalk of celery, but you also may find a bevy of pickled vegetables and (it being Wisconsin) cheese, of course. And what would a Wisconsin Mary be without beef jerky or sausages? Also, don't forget the shrimp. Or a chicken leg. And a cheeseburger? Yes, you read that correctly! A Northwoods Mary is a complete meal, artfully balanced over a chilled, spicy beverage, accompanied by a snit!

CT's Deli in Rhinelander makes what they call the "Lunchbox Bloody Mary," which should be included in *Ripley's Believe It or Not.* Served in a pitcher, the Lunchbox Bloody Mary is for two to four

Up North we take our Bloody Marys seriously. CT'S DELI.

people and includes five-ounce beer chasers for all and a staggering cascade of lunch treats—four smoked chicken wings, four smoked beef ribs, beef sticks, pepperoni, pepperjack and cheddar cheeses, pickles, olives, mushrooms, and pretzel rods with beer cheese dip.

Every New Year's Eve Day between 10 a.m. and 3 p.m., CT's has an event called "Daydrinking," where they offer the Lunchbox Bloody Mary (which normally costs $39) for the cost of the year . . . $20.23, $20.24. Chef Tom and Rhonda Jicinsky, owners of CT's, say they make close to one hundred Lunchbox Marys for that event every year. "It's so fun to see Lunchboxes all over the deli," says Rhonda. They scour thrift stores all year long, looking for cheap beer pitchers, which they collect for the event. (Patrons get to keep their Bloody Mary pitcher and take it home.)

Although CT's Lunchbox Bloody Mary recipe remains a closely guarded secret, you can try this Up North Loaded Bloody Mary and create your own "Lunchbox" creation.

Up North Loaded Bloody Mary

Triple this recipe to do a pitcher version of a loaded Bloody Mary, or double the recipe and pour mix into ice cube trays. Frozen Bloody Mary mix cubes will not dilute the drink like regular ice cubes do.

16 ounces tomato juice

1 tablespoon creamy horseradish

1 tablespoon Worcestershire sauce

½ teaspoon dill pickle juice

¾ teaspoon celery salt

1 teaspoon garlic salt

Freshly ground black pepper

Tabasco sauce (optional)

Bloody Mary mix ice cubes

4 ounces vodka

2 lemon wedges (optional)

Garnishes of choice

At least 2 hours ahead: Mix together tomato juice, horseradish, Worcestershire sauce, pickle juice, celery salt, garlic salt, and freshly ground black pepper to taste. Season with Tabasco sauce to taste, if desired. Refrigerate until serving.

Fill 2 glasses with Bloody Mary mix ice cubes. Add 2 ounces vodka to each glass and fill glass with Bloody Mary mix. Add a squeeze of lemon if desired. Garnish with a potpourri of toppings.

(SERVES 2)

Mango Tango Summer Cooler

This is a refreshing light cocktail for a hot summer day. To make sure melting ice cubes do not water down the drink, freeze Cran-Mango juice in ice-cube trays and use them instead of regular cubes.

1 (750 mL) bottle Stella Rosa white wine, mango or pineapple flavored

1 cup mango vodka

½ cup banana liqueur

1½ cups Ocean Spray Cran-Mango juice

24 ounces Zevia lemon-lime soda

Early in the day: Combine wine, vodka, liqueur, and juice in a 10-cup pitcher or divide ingredients between 2 smaller pitchers. Stir to combine. Refrigerate until ready to serve.

To serve: Stir lemon-lime soda into wine mixture. (If using 2 pitchers, add 12 ounces soda to each.) Fill short tumblers halfway with ice and fill glass with Mango Tango.

Chef's note: You can substitute mango rum for the mango vodka. Be sure to use sugar-free lemon-lime soda, like Zevia, or the drink will be too sweet.

(SERVES 10 TO 12)

Peartini Irene

My dear friend Irene enjoyed this drink every night, lovingly made by her husband, Tom, right up to the day she died in 2022. This one's for you, girl!

3 slices thinly sliced ripe pear

1 ounce Absolut Pears vodka

1 ounce St. Germain Elderflower liqueur

1 thin slice lemon peel, for garnishing

Rim a martini glass with a slice of pear, twice around. Put remaining 2 pear slices in the glass. Combine pear-flavored vodka and elderflower liqueur in a cocktail shaker with ice cubes and shake until foamy. Strain into the prepared glass. Garnish with lemon peel and serve.

(SERVES 1)

Sangria

Always a hit at summer outdoor gatherings, this fruity sangria recipe can be doubled or tripled to serve a crowd. The drink should be made one day ahead so that flavors can marry.

1 bottle Syrah or other dry red wine of choice

1 lemon, juiced and strained

1 lime, juiced and strained

1 orange, juiced and strained

¼ cup pineapple juice

2 tablespoons sugar

3 ounces gin (2 shots)

½ cup thinly sliced fresh pineapple

1 cup thinly sliced fresh or frozen strawberries

3 cups ginger ale

One day ahead: Place wine, juices, sugar, gin, and pineapple slices in a large pitcher. Stir until sugar is dissolved. Cover and refrigerate overnight.

To serve: Stir strawberries and ginger ale into sangria. Serve in ice-filled tall wineglasses.

(SERVES 8 TO 10)

Mercer Moonshine

3 ounces Deep Eddy Ruby Red grapefruit-flavored vodka

6 ounces grapefruit juice

1½ ounces cranberry juice

Combine vodka and juices in an ice-filled cocktail shaker. Shake well and strain into a martini glass.

(SERVES 1)

Call of the Loon

Just as distinctive as the ubiquitous call of Up North loons, which inhabit virtually every lake, the crucial ingredient in this killer punch is orgeat syrup, a sweet syrup made from almonds, sugar, and rose or orange-flower water. Substituting almond syrup makes this drink taste almost the same.

12 ounces pineapple juice (1½ cups)

16 ounces orange juice

2 dashes Angostura bitters

2 ounces grenadine

12 ounces white rum

½ ounce Myers dark rum

2 ounces orgeat or almond syrup

Up to 1 week ahead: In a large pitcher, mix together pineapple juice, orange juice, bitters, grenadine, white and dark rums, and almond syrup in a large pitcher. Stir to combine. Refrigerate until ready to serve. Serve each drink in a tall glass filled with ice cubes.

(SERVES 8)

Every lake has a pair of resident loons. SHUTTERSTOCK

Tom and Jerry—Definitely Not a Cat-and-Mouse Game

"Christmas in a mug" aptly describes this quintessential Wisconsin wintertime hot drink—the Tom and Jerry. Not to be confused with eggnog, the Tom and Jerry is a concoction of whipped egg batter, powdered sugar, nutmeg, and a shot of both rum and brandy, mixed with a little hot water. Creamy and smooth, with a slightly foamy top, the Tom and Jerry usually makes its debut in November, when the weather gets cold, and is a drink of choice until the snow thaws.

Where did this classic drink get its name? Definitely not from a cartoon cat named Tom and a mouse named Jerry. An English bartender named Jerry Thomas claimed he invented the drink in 1847 and named it after himself. But cocktail historian Wayne Curtis said the Tom and Jerry recipe first appeared in print in England before Thomas was even born. According to Curtis, the drink was invented in 1821 as a promotional drink that was served to theatergoers who came to see the British production of *Tom and Jerry, or Life in London*. The play and the drink were wildly popular. The play came to America in 1823 and more than likely the promotional cocktail did too.

How the Tom and Jerry landed in Wisconsin is anybody's guess, but it stuck, becoming an iconic holiday libation. Local bars and restaurants start serving the drink around Thanksgiving, at which time premade Tom and Jerry batter—Connolly's and Mama Bowen's—becomes available in regional supermarkets. That said, the best and most available Tom and Jerry batter is homemade.

Tom and Jerry Cocktail

This recipe has been in my family for generations. My parents even had a set of Tom and Jerry Christmas mugs in which they served the eggnoggy cocktail.

2 extra-large pasteurized eggs, separated

4 tablespoons powdered sugar

Brandy

Myers dark rum

Boiling water

Freshly grated nutmeg, for garnishing

To make batter: In a medium bowl, beat egg whites with an electric mixer until stiff. Beat in powdered sugar gradually. In a separate bowl, beat egg yolks until they are thin. Fold yolks into whites.

To make the drinks: Spoon a generous tablespoon of batter into each mug. (Amount will depend on the size of the mug.) Add a jigger of brandy and a half-jigger of rum. Add hot water to fill mug ¾ full. Stir gently. (A slight foam should form on top.) Top with freshly grated nutmeg and serve.

(SERVES 2 TO 3)

Hot Mulled Cider

Look for fresh apple cider at farmers' markets during apple season in the autumn months. (See Bayfield Fruit Loop sidebar, page 184.)

½ gallon (64 ounces) apple cider

½ teaspoon whole cloves

Dash ground nutmeg

¼ cup brown sugar

½ teaspoon whole allspice

1 (3-inch) cinnamon stick

Place cider, cloves, nutmeg, brown sugar, allspice, and cinnamon stick in a large nonstick saucepan over high heat. Bring to a boil. Reduce heat to low and simmer, uncovered, for 10 minutes. Pour cider mixture through a strainer into a large heat-proof bowl. Discard spices. Serve immediately in ceramic mugs or transfer to a covered container and refrigerate until needed. Serve cold or reheat cider in a large nonstick saucepan over low heat before serving.

(SERVES 8)

SHUTTERSTOCK

Summertime Lemonade

Nothing says summer like a tall glass of fresh-squeezed lemonade. Or try an Arnold Palmer—half lemonade, half iced tea.

1½ cups sugar

½ cup water

1 tablespoon grated lemon peel

1½ cups fresh squeezed lemon juice

5 cups water

Mint sprigs

Place sugar and water in a medium saucepan over medium-high heat. Bring to a boil, then reduce heat to medium-low and simmer until sugar has completely dissolved, about 2 minutes. Transfer this sugar syrup to a large pitcher.

Add lemon peel, lemon juice, and water. Stir to combine. Refrigerate until cold. Serve over ice in tall glasses garnished with a mint sprig.

(SERVES 8)

The Brandy Old Fashioned

The Brandy Old Fashioned, Wisconsin's unofficial state cocktail, most likely rose in popularity during the bootleg Prohibition days. To mask the taste of low-quality booze, the concoction featured muddled sugar, fruit, and soda, to the point that some bartenders called it a fruit salad!

The quality of liquor improved after Prohibition was repealed, but the "fruit salad" drink remained popular. After World War II, the quality of booze took another dive due to the fact that grain had been shipped to Europe in the preceding years rather than made into liquor. It was then that Wisconsin liquor distributors discovered that Christian Brothers Brandy had about 30,000 cases of aged brandy on hand, and the distributors purchased it all. Wisconsinites were hooked! Brandy replaced whiskey in their favored Old Fashioned, and the Brandy Old Fashioned soared to new heights of popularity.

Today, Wisconsin consumes half of Korbel's annual brandy supply. No two Old Fashioneds are made exactly alike. They all have sugar cubes muddled with an orange wedge, a couple of dashes of bitters, ice, and brandy, of course. But then, you'll need to choose how you want it: Brandy Old Fashioned Sweet is topped with lemon-lime soda and maybe a little maraschino cherry juice. Brandy Old Fashioned Sour uses a sour soda like Squirt. Brandy Old Fashioned Soda is made with seltzer water. Brandy Old Fashioned Press is topped with half seltzer and half lemon-lime soda. The cocktail is traditionally garnished with another wedge of orange and a maraschino cherry. Sometimes you'll even find the drink garnished with a skewer of olives or pickled vegetables, like onions or Brussels sprouts. However, don't expect to find a Brandy Old Fashioned out of the state. An Old Fashioned is quite another glass of hooch in the other forty-nine!

Brandy Old Fashioned

1 sugar cube

2 dashes Angostura bitters

2 ounces brandy

2 orange slices, divided

2 maraschino cherries, divided

1 to 2 ounces lemon-lime soda, sour soda, seltzer, or 50/50 lemon-lime soda and seltzer

Place sugar cube in the bottom of a short tumbler or rocks glass. Add dashes of bitters atop sugar cubes. Add a drop of brandy atop sugar cube (just enough to dissolve the sugar cube).

Add one orange slice and a maraschino cherry. Gently muddle to crush the fruit but not pulverize it. Fill the glass with ice cubes. Add the brandy. Top off with soda of choice. Give it a stir and garnish with another orange wedge and another cherry.

(SERVES 1)

Which end is up? Clouds are reflected in an Up North lake. GETTY IMAGES

Soup's On!

Aunt Rita's Tried-and-True Two-Bean Chili

I found this recipe on a yellowed, well-splattered card in an old recipe file that belonged to my mother. Her younger sister's chili lives up to its tried-and-true boast. It is the best I've ever tasted.

1 teaspoon olive oil

1 cup chopped sweet onions, like Vidalia

1 pound ground beef (90 percent lean)

3 teaspoons garlic paste or finely minced garlic

½ cup chopped green bell pepper

1 (14.5-ounce) can stewed tomatoes with onions, celery, and green peppers

1 (14.5-ounce) can stewed tomatoes with basil, garlic, and oregano

2 teaspoons instant bouillon dissolved in 2 cups boiling water or 2 cups beef broth

1 (8-ounce) can tomato sauce

1 tablespoon chili powder

1 teaspoon salt

1 teaspoon ground cumin

⅛ teaspoon cayenne pepper

1 (15-ounce) can black beans, rinsed and drained

1 (15.8-ounce) can Great Northern beans, rinsed and drained

Place olive oil in a large soup pot over medium heat. Add onions, ground beef, and garlic. Cook, stirring frequently, until onions are soft and beef is almost cooked through, about 3½ minutes. Add bell peppers and cook, stirring frequently, for 1½ minutes more. Add stewed tomatoes with their juices, bouillon mixture, tomato sauce, chili powder, salt, cumin, cayenne pepper, and beans. Stir to combine ingredients.

Bring to a boil, then reduce heat to low and simmer, uncovered, for 45 minutes, stirring occasionally.

(MAKES 8 CUPS)

"BLT" Soup

With all the flavors of the classic sandwich that bears the same initials, this "BLT" is made with bacon, leek, and tomato. Leeks are in the same family as onions and garlic. Their stalks are composed of layers of leaf sheaths. Dirt tends to get caught between the sheaths, so be sure to rinse them thoroughly.

2 tablespoons butter

1 leek, white parts only, washed well, dried with paper toweling, and thinly sliced

3 strips center-cut bacon, diced

2 pounds ripe plum tomatoes, peeled, seeded, and diced

1 teaspoon fresh thyme or ½ teaspoon dried

¼ teaspoon onion powder

¼ teaspoon garlic powder

¼ teaspoon salt, plus more

⅛ teaspoon black pepper, plus more

2 bay leaves

4 cups (32 ounces) chicken broth

½ cup heavy cream or sour cream, for serving

Melt butter in a large nonstick saucepan over medium heat. Add sliced leeks and diced bacon and cook until bacon is crispy, about 2 minutes. Add tomatoes, thyme, onion and garlic powders, salt, pepper, and bay leaves. Sauté for 5 minutes, stirring frequently.

Add broth. Bring to a boil on high. Reduce heat to low and simmer for 20 minutes, stirring occasionally.

Remove bay leaves and puree soup in batches in a blender. (Hold a kitchen towel over top of blender so hot liquid does not splatter and burn you.) Add salt and pepper to taste. Return soup to saucepan and keep it warm on low until ready to serve.

To serve: Drizzle each serving with a little heavy cream or top each serving with a small dollop of sour cream.

(SERVES 6)

Butternut Squash–Pear Soup

Butternut squash is so rich and pure that it doesn't need much window dressing to take a starring role at the dinner table, but the Bosc pears are the supporting actors in this version of butternut squash soup.

1 tablespoon butter

1 teaspoon garlic paste or minced garlic

½ cup chopped sweet onions, like Vidalia

2 pounds butternut squash, seeded, peeled, and cut into ½-inch dice

3 unripe firm Bosc pears, peeled, cored, and chopped

1 teaspoon gingerroot paste or minced gingerroot

½ teaspoon salt

⅛ teaspoon black pepper

Dash allspice

2 cups chicken broth

Sour cream, for serving

Melt butter in a large soup pot over medium heat. Add garlic and onions and sauté, stirring frequently, for 2 minutes. Add squash, pears, gingerroot, salt, pepper, allspice, and broth. Increase heat to high. Bring to a boil. Reduce heat to low, cover pot, and simmer until squash is fork-tender, about 5 minutes.

Remove from heat and puree with an immersion stick blender or puree in batches in a blender. Return soup to pot. Simmer on low for another minute, or until soup is hot. Serve topped with a dollop of sour cream.

(SERVES 4)

In the Beginning . . . The Ojibwe Nation

Paleo Indians arrived in what is now Wisconsin about 12,000 years ago, after the retreat of the last continental glacier. By the time the first European explorers reached the region in the 1600s, several Native American groups were living there. The Ojibwe nation settled in the northern portions of Wisconsin.

The Ojibwe (to European ears this sounded like "Chippewa," which they are also called today) were hunter/gatherers. Life followed the seasons. In the early spring, they tapped maple trees and made syrup and maple sugar. They planted gardens of corn, beans, squash, and potatoes in the late spring. In the summer, the men hunted and fished, while the women gathered wild vegetables, like onions and leeks, as well as berries and herbs. They also tended the gardens. The produce was dried and stored in birchbark bags. Meat was cut into thick strips, wound around sticks, and then smoked over an open fire.

In the fall, they harvested wild rice, an immensely important staple of their diet. (See sidebar, page 160.) Produce from the gardens was dried and stored in pits or caves that were lined with birchbark. Migrating pigeons were caught in stringed nets suspended on

Early Ojibwe (Chippewa) build a canoe. GETTY IMAGES

poles. Winter was deer-hunting time for the men, who also trapped beaver, otter, and other fur-bearing animals. They also cut holes in ice-topped lakes and spear-fished for muskie and pike. The women made clothes for the family.

French explorer Jean Nicolet was probably the first European to encounter the Ojibwe, when he entered northern Wisconsin in 1634. The Ojibwe welcomed the Frenchmen, who subsequently arrived and fought alongside them against the British. (The area was under French control until 1763, when the British acquired it.) Americans quickly started encroaching upon the area over the ensuing decades. Throughout the 1800s, through treaties and military defeats, the United States dispossessed the Ojibwe of nearly two-thirds of present-day northern Wisconsin as well as a portion of central Minnesota and much of the upper peninsula of Michigan. In 1854, in the last treaty between the tribe and the US government, four reservations were created: Bad River Band, Lac Courte Oreilles Band, Lac du Flambeau Band, and Red Cliff Band. Mole Lake Band and St. Croix Band were formed later. Of the millions of acres that the Ojibwe considered their homeland, less than 275,000 acres remained.

Did You Know?

- Frog Bay, the first tribal national park in the United States, was established by the Red Cliff Band in Bayfield. The 90-acre park, a boreal forest, hugs the Lake Superior shoreline overlooking the Apostle Islands.
- All six bands now have casinos. Revenues go to the tribes and benefit the community.
- Red Cliff Band operates a walleye and trout fish hatchery.
- Every year the bands reseed more than six tons of wild rice into dozens of existing wild rice beds.
- Lac du Flambeau reservation is the location of Strawberry Island, recognized by the National Register of Historical Places. It is the site of the last battle between the Sioux and the Ojibwe in 1745. An archeological survey in 1966 identified artifacts dating back to 200 B.C.

French Onion Soup

The secret to a great French onion soup is in the broth, not in the thick crusty bread and oozing cheese topping so often found in restaurants. In this recipe, the sweet flavor of slow-cooked caramelized onions shines through a delicately seasoned broth. The Gruyère croutes hide undercover, soaking up the flavors of the soup and offering a cheesy bonus.

6 large sweet onions, like Vidalia, peeled, cut in half, and thinly sliced

½ cup melted butter

1 teaspoon sugar

½ cup dry sherry

4 cups beef broth

2 cups chicken broth

1 teaspoon snipped fresh thyme or ⅓ teaspoon dried

1 teaspoon snipped fresh flat-leaf parsley or ⅓ teaspoon dried

½ teaspoon salt

¼ teaspoon pepper

1 small (9-ounce) baguette, cut into 1-inch slices (about 16 slices)

2 cloves garlic, peeled and halved

1 tablespoon Dijon mustard

1½ cups shredded Gruyère or Swiss cheese

Twelve hours ahead: Place onions in a 6-quart slow cooker. Pour melted butter over onions. Cover and cook on low setting for 9½ to 10 hours, until onions have caramelized.

Place sugar in a large bowl. Add sherry and whisk until sugar is dissolved. Add beef and chicken broths, thyme, parsley, salt, and pepper. Whisk until well combined. Pour broth mixture into slow cooker. Stir with onions to mix well. Cook on low setting for 2 hours.

While soup is cooking, make the Gruyère croutes. Preheat oven to 300 degrees F. Place baguette slices on a nonstick baking sheet. Bake for 15 minutes. Remove from oven. Rub cut side of each half-clove of garlic over the top of 4 baguette slices. Spread a thin layer of mustard over each baguette slice. Top each slice with an equal amount of cheese, packing it into a tight mound. Bake croutes for 5 minutes or until cheese has melted.

To serve: Ladle 1½ cups onion soup in each bowl. Tuck 2 Gruyère croutes into the soup in each bowl so that only the cheesy tops are exposed. Serve immediately.

Chef's note: The raw onions will fill the slow cooker to the brim, but don't worry; they cook down to a quarter of the volume as they caramelize.

(SERVES 8.)

Gingered Carrot Vichyssoise

Whereas the Irish may lay claim to hearty potato soup, the origin of vichyssoise—potato and leek soup served cold—is hotly debated between France and America. This version, however, is a fusion of many cultures. The addition of carrots, orange juice, and ginger-root to the vichyssoise adds a subtle Asian influence to the mix.

1 tablespoon olive oil

1 teaspoon garlic paste or finely minced garlic

1½ tablespoons gingerroot paste or finely minced gingerroot

1 leek, white part only, halved, washed well, and thinly sliced

8 large carrots, peeled and sliced into 1-inch-thick pieces

2 large Yukon Gold potatoes, peeled, halved lengthwise, and cut into 1-inch-thick pieces

2 bay leaves

½ cup orange juice

6½ cups (52 ounces) chicken broth

½ cup white wine

1 teaspoon salt

½ teaspoon black pepper

1 cup heavy cream

Snipped fresh chives, for serving

One day ahead: Place oil in a large nonstick skillet over medium-low heat. Add garlic, gingerroot, and leeks and sauté for 3 minutes, until leeks are soft. Transfer to a 4-quart slow cooker. Add carrots, pota-toes, bay leaves, orange juice, chicken broth, wine, salt, and pepper to the slow cooker. Stir to combine. Cover slow cooker and cook on low setting for 8 to 9 hours, until carrots and potatoes are soft.

Remove bay leaves. Transfer soup to a blender and puree in batches. Transfer to a large, covered con-tainer. Stir in cream, cover, and refrigerate until soup is completely chilled.

To serve: Stir soup and ladle it into large, shallow soup bowls. Sprinkle each serving with chives.

Chef's note: You can serve this soup chilled or warm. To reheat, place soup in a large nonstick saucepan over low heat until it is heated through. (Do not allow soup to come to a boil.)

(MAKES 12 CUPS)

Mushroom Soup

This soup is exquisite with ordinary button and baby bella mushrooms, but you can jazz it up with a combination that includes more exotic mushrooms, such as Portobello, shiitake, cremini, or porcini if you'd like.

1 tablespoon olive oil

2 pounds baby bella and/or white button mushrooms, wiped clean and thinly sliced

1 cup chopped sweet onions, like Vidalia

2 tablespoons fresh lemon juice

2 tablespoons dark brown sugar

1½ teaspoons dried thyme leaves

⅓ cup white wine

1 (14-ounce) can vegetable broth (2 cups)

1 (32-ounce) carton chicken broth (4 cups)

1 teaspoon salt

½ teaspoon black pepper

Busha Browne's Pepper Sherry or cream sherry, for serving

Place olive oil in a large nonstick skillet over medium heat. Add mushrooms, onions, lemon juice, brown sugar, and thyme. Sauté for 5 minutes, stirring frequently, until mushrooms have softened and any released liquid has evaporated. Add white wine and cook for 5 minutes more.

Transfer mushroom mixture to a large saucepan over medium heat. Add vegetable and chicken broths, salt, and pepper. Bring mixture to a boil, then reduce heat to low. Cover and simmer for 30 minutes, stirring occasionally.

Remove 1 cup mushrooms from soup with a slotted spoon and set aside. Transfer soup to a blender and puree (in batches if necessary) until smooth. (Hold a kitchen towel over top of blender so hot liquid does not splatter and burn you.) Return soup to saucepan. Stir in reserved mushrooms. Place saucepan over low heat until soup is hot. Divide soup among 6 bowls and serve with sherry on the side.

(SERVES 6)

You're Invited to the Booyah

Perhaps reminiscent of the one-pot meal the Ojibwe (Chippewa) tribes shared with French fur traders around a campfire in northern Wisconsin's early pre-statehood days, booyah is a sharing event. Believed to have been introduced to northeastern Wisconsin by Belgian immigrants, this everything-but-the-kitchen-sink stew of chicken, meat, and vegetables has reached legendary status.

Popular at fall community gatherings, church picnics, and family reunions, booyah can take up to two days and multiple cooks to prepare. It is traditionally long-simmered in enormous, specially designed, steel or cast-iron "booyah kettles," outdoors over a wood-burning fire, often in twenty- to fifty-gallon batches.

To not confuse the issue, allow me to clarify: Booyah is the name of the dish that is served as well as the name of the event get-together itself. So, "come to my booyah for booyah!"

Slow Cooker Booyah

I'm guessing that most home cooks don't have a fifty-gallon booyah kettle hovering over their backyard firepit, so try making this nearly authentic booyah in your slow cooker.

1 pound boneless, skinless chicken breasts

¾ pound beef stew meat

1½ teaspoons kosher salt, plus more

1 teaspoon black pepper, plus more

1 tablespoon plus 1 teaspoon olive oil, divided

1 cup chopped onions

4 cups chicken broth, divided

1 teaspoon garlic powder

2 teaspoons McCormick's Citrus Grill, or lemon-spice-herb seasoning of choice

1 cup diced celery

1 cup diced baby carrots

1 pound peeled, diced potatoes

1 can diced tomatoes in basil and garlic

1 bay leaf

2 teaspoons Worcestershire sauce

1 teaspoon soy sauce

1 cup frozen peas

1 cup frozen corn

1 cup chopped salad mix

Oyster crackers, for serving

Season chicken and beef liberally with salt and pepper. In a large skillet, heat 1 tablespoon oil over medium-high heat. Add chicken and brown on all sides. Remove chicken from pan. Add beef and brown on all sides. Remove beef. Add remaining 1 teaspoon oil to pan. Add onions and cook until they brown slightly. Transfer chicken, beef, and onions to a large slow cooker. Add 2 cups chicken broth. Stir in kosher salt, pepper, garlic powder, and citrus seasoning. Cook on high for 3 hours. Shred beef and chicken.

Add celery, carrots, potatoes, diced tomatoes with their juices, remaining 2 cups chicken broth, bay leaf, Worcestershire sauce, and soy sauce to slow cooker. Stir to combine. Cook on low for 2 hours. Add peas, corn, and chopped salad to slow cooker and cook for 1 hour more or until potatoes and vegetables are tender. Remove bay leaf before serving. Serve with oyster crackers.

(SERVES 8 TO 10)

Pasta e Fagioli

One of Italy's most beloved soups, this bean and pasta soup is a hearty meal in and of itself. Serve with fresh Italian bread and a salad of fruit or leafy greens.

8 ounces (about 1¼ cups) dried Great Northern beans

¼ pound salt pork, finely diced

2 cups chopped sweet onions, like Vidalia

1 (14.5-ounce) can petite-cut tomatoes with garlic and olive oil

2 teaspoons garlic paste or finely minced garlic

2 teaspoons instant beef bouillon granules

5 cups water

½ teaspoon coarse kosher salt

¼ teaspoon cracked black pepper

1 cup ditalini pasta or miniature shells, bows, or elbow macaroni

One day ahead: Place dried beans in a large bowl. Add water to cover beans by 3 inches. Allow beans to soak at room temperature overnight.

Early in the day: Drain beans in a colander. Rinse and drain again. Place beans in a 4-quart slow cooker. Place salt pork in a large nonstick skillet over medium heat. Cook pork, stirring constantly, for 2 minutes. Remove pork with a slotted spoon and drain on paper toweling. Add pork to slow cooker. Add onions to skillet and sauté until translucent, about 3 minutes. Transfer onions to slow cooker.

Drain tomatoes in a sieve, reserving juices (about ½ cup). Add tomatoes to slow cooker. Whisk garlic into reserved tomato juice and add to slow cooker. Dissolve beef bouillon granules in water. Add to slow cooker. Add salt and pepper and stir until all ingredients are well combined.

Cover slow cooker and cook on low setting for 8 hours, until beans are al dente. Add pasta to slow cooker and cook 30 to 45 minutes more, until pasta is al dente and beans are tender.

(SERVES 6)

Out of Hand

The Pasty—A Taste of Up North History

The first mineral rush in the United States, in the 1830s, happened in southwestern Wisconsin. The discovery attracted experienced miners from Cornwall, England, who worked these mines for a time. When the resources began to deplete, they moved northward to work the underground iron and copper mines in the Gogebic Iron Range, an eighty-mile-long belt of Precambian bedrock in northern Wisconsin and the Upper Peninsula of Michigan.

The Cornish miners' most famous contribution to the gustatory culture of Up North Wisconsin is the pasty—a baked, handheld, pocket-sized savory meat and vegetable dinner pie that they took with them in a tin bucket to work. The D-shaped pie—its crust crimped along the curved edge—could be easily carried and could be eaten without cutlery. Furthermore, its dense, folded crust stayed warm for hours and could easily be reheated over a candle or gas lantern deep in the mine. The Finnish and Swedish miners who followed adopted the meat pie as their own and cemented the pasty as a star in the regional culture.

The pasty's ubiquitous crimped crust has inspired a few legends over the centuries. It is said that the miners used the crust as a sort of handle, throwing away the wide, crimped edges after eating the pasty to avoid being poisoned by the tin, iron, or copper dust that might have clung to their dirty fingers. But a long-fabled superstition in the mining culture provided another explanation: The mines were inhabited by the spirits of dead miners, which the miners called "tommyknockers." They believed the knockers would play tricks on them, such as move tools around or hide things. To keep the knockers happy, the miners would leave the pasty crusts as an offering, thereby appeasing the lurking spirits.

A Cornish pasty (pronounced *PAST-ee*—sounds like past, not paste) was filled with beef (typically beef skirt steak), onions, potatoes, and rutabagas, all cut into very small cubes and placed, uncooked, atop the lower half of a circle of pie crust. The upper half of the crust circle was then folded over and the curved edges firmly crimped to provide a tight seal. The top of the pasty was brushed with egg wash, a small slit cut in the top of the crust to release the steam, and the pie was slowly baked until golden brown. The filling and the crust baked at the same rate. (To be deemed a "genuine Cornish pasty," the Cornish Pasty Association requires the pasty must be a D shape with crimping along the curve and a minimum of 12.5 percent meat and 25 percent vegetables—no meat except beef, no vegetables other than potatoes, rutabagas, and onions!)

But today, Up North, you'll find a myriad of fillings tucked inside our pasties. The traditional pasty now dictates ground beef (undoubtedly the Scandinavian influence), potatoes, and onions, but you'll still find rutabaga in the Cornish-style pasties. Family-owned and -operated for generations, Joe's Pasty Shop has been making authentic pasties since 1946, with shops in Rhinelander as well as just over the Wisconsin-Michigan border in Ironwood, Michigan. Be it a pizza pasty, Greek pasty, or hatch green chili chicken pasty, the fillings are limited only by imagination. As the owner of Joe's states, "It's a very familiar, memorable food for people. They are really passionate about their favorite pasty."

Up North Pasties

1 tablespoon olive oil, divided

1½ cups chopped onions, like Vidalia

3 cups diced (¼-inch) potatoes, like Yukon Gold

1 pound ground beef

1 pound ground pork

Seasoned salt

Freshly ground black pepper

2 (15-ounce) packages rolled Pillsbury pie crusts (2 in each package), at room temperature

1 large egg, beaten with 1 tablespoon water

Ketchup, for serving

Up to 1 month ahead: Place 2 teaspoons olive oil in a large nonstick skillet over medium heat. When oil is hot, add onions and potatoes and sauté, stirring frequently, until onions are soft, about 2½ minutes. Transfer mixture to a large bowl.

Place remaining 1 teaspoon olive oil in skillet. Add ground beef and cook, stirring frequently, until meat is browned. With a slotted spoon, transfer beef to a bowl. Add ground pork to skillet and cook, stirring frequently, until browned. Transfer pork to bowl with a slotted spoon. Sprinkle with seasoned salt and freshly ground black pepper to taste. Stir to mix well. Set aside.

Place 1 pie crust atop a large piece of parchment paper. Roll dough with a rolling pin until it is large enough to cut two 7-inch circles of dough. (Use

SHUTTERSTOCK

a saucepan lid as your template and cut around the edge with a sharp paring knife.) Place ½-cup meat mixture in the lower half of each circle. Bring other side of dough circle over filling, creating a half-moon. Crimp the edges of the dough into a firm seam. Cut 3 small steam vents in the top of the pasty and place it on a parchment-paper-lined baking sheet.

Repeat this process with remaining 3 pie crusts, reserving cut-away dough. Form cut-away dough into a ball and roll it out, cutting as many 7-inch circles of dough as you can and repeating the filling/crimping process. Place trays of pasties in the freezer until frozen solid. Transfer them to a large, covered container. Separate layers with waxed paper. Freeze until needed.

To bake: Preheat oven to 400 degrees F. Defrost pasties to room temperature on a nonstick baking sheet that has been lightly coated with vegetable cooking spray. Brush tops of pasties with egg wash. Bake for 20 to 25 minutes, until crust is golden brown and filling has heated through. Serve with a side of ketchup.

Chef's note: You can use all ground beef in the pasties if you wish. I like to use 4S Seasoning Salt, which I order online from the Wisconsin spice company, Penzey's (www.penzeys.com), but any seasoned salt will work in this recipe.

(MAKES 12 PASTIES)

Hot Super Sub

Italian immigrants to America made a traditional sandwich consisting of a long loaf of bread filled with cold cuts and topped with a salad of lettuce, tomatoes, onions, olive oil, vinegar, salt, pepper, and Italian spices. A New York City grocer, who sold the sandwiches in 1910, reportedly named them submarines because the shape of the bread reminded him of naval subs.

½ stick butter, room temperature

1 tablespoon Dijon mustard

1 tablespoon snipped fresh parsley or ½ teaspoon dried

1 large clove garlic, crushed and minced

¼ teaspoon crushed red pepper flakes

1 loaf Italian bread, sliced in half lengthwise

¼ pound thinly sliced deli ham

¼ pound thinly sliced salami

¼ pound thinly sliced large pepperoni

1 medium sweet onion, like Vidalia, thinly sliced

1 (12-ounce) jar mild banana-pepper rings

2 medium tomatoes, thinly sliced

6 ounces Muenster cheese, thinly sliced

Preheat oven to 400 degrees F. Combine butter, mustard, parsley, garlic, and red pepper flakes in a small bowl. Spread entire butter mixture on cut sides of top and bottom of the bread. On the bottom slice of bread, layer ingredients—ham, salami, pepperoni, onions, pepper rings, tomatoes, cheese—in order. Put top half of bread over ingredients, forming a sandwich. Wrap tightly in several layers of aluminum foil. Place on a baking sheet and bake for 20 to 25 minutes, until cheese melts. Cut into 6 to 8 pieces and serve hot.

Chef's note: If you keep the baked sandwich wrapped in several layers of foil and then wrap it in a dish towel, it will stay hot for a couple of hours. This is great fare to take out in the boat or on a picnic.

(SERVES 6 TO 8)

Grilled Five-Cheese Sandwiches

My mother always called grilled cheese sandwiches "cheese toastwiches," which, as a child, I thought were very special. This version redefines the classic, following the self-indulgent concept that, like chocolate and jewelry, one can never have too much cheese.

FOR THE FILLING:

1 cup shredded cheddar cheese

1 cup shredded Monterey Jack cheese

1 cup shredded Swiss cheese

1 (3-ounce) package cream cheese, softened

¼ cup mayonnaise

¼ teaspoon garlic powder

2 teaspoons Dijon mustard

FOR EACH SANDWICH:

2 slices white, sourdough, or whole grain bread

1 tablespoon salted butter, room temperature

1 tablespoon Parmesan cheese

To make the filling: Mix together cheddar, Jack, Swiss, and cream cheeses in a medium bowl. Add mayonnaise, garlic powder, and mustard. Stir until ingredients are well mixed.

To make each sandwich: Spread about ¼-cup cheese filling atop one bread slice. Top with the other bread slice. Butter each of the two sides of sandwich. Sprinkle each with Parmesan cheese.

Place a nonstick skillet over medium-low heat for 30 seconds. Place sandwich in skillet and cook for 3 minutes. Flip sandwich with a firm spatula. Cook for 1½ minutes, until golden brown. Flip sandwich one more time, press down on sandwich with spatula, and cook for 30 seconds longer. Remove sandwich from skillet, cut it on the diagonal, and serve immediately.

Chef's note: You can refrigerate filling in a covered container for up to 1 month. Be sure to cook the sandwich on medium-low heat, so that the cheese has a chance to melt before bread gets too browned.

(MAKES 10 SANDWICHES)

Butter Burger Sliders

Butter burgers are quintessentially Wisconsin. It is considered de rigueur to butter and toast the bun and place a dab of butter atop the freshly grilled burger. I've taken these baby burgers, commonly called sliders, one step further by seasoning them from the inside, not the outside, in three different ways: portobello, onion, and Swiss; blue cheese; and cheddar and bacon.

2½ pounds ground beef (90 percent lean)

2 slices bacon, cut into small dice

⅓ cup finely chopped Portobello mushrooms

¼ cup finely chopped sweet onions, like Vidalia

¼ cup shredded Swiss cheese

⅓ cup crumbled blue cheese

⅓ cup shredded cheddar cheese

Salt and freshly ground black pepper

1 (12-count) package slider rolls or other 3-inch-diameter round rolls

4 tablespoons soft butter

Roma tomatoes, for serving

Baby lettuce, for serving

Toppings of choice, for serving

Divide ground beef into three equal portions and place in separate medium bowls. Cook bacon in a medium nonstick skillet over medium heat until bacon is cooked through but not crispy. Remove from heat and drain.

While bacon is cooking, mix mushrooms, onions, and Swiss cheese with ground beef in one bowl. Mix blue cheese with ground beef in the second bowl. Mix bacon and cheddar cheese with ground beef in the third bowl.

Using a 3-inch-diameter round biscuit ring, form burger patties with your clean hands. Divide beef mixture in each bowl into 4 equal portions. Press beef into ring to form a patty that is 1 inch thick. Repeat with beef mixtures in the remaining two bowls. (You'll have 12 patties, 4 of each variety, 3 inches in diameter and 1 inch thick.) Season burgers with salt and pepper to taste. Butter cut sides of top and bottom slider buns.

Preheat outdoor grill to 475 degrees F. Cook burgers for about 4 minutes. Flip burgers and cook 4 minutes more for medium-rare. Check doneness by cutting into one burger with a knife. Adjust timing for rare or medium burgers. Toast buttered buns briefly on grill rack.

To serve: Place burgers on the bottom slider buns. Place a dab of butter on each burger before adding the top buns. Serve with sliced Roma tomatoes and baby lettuce, along with traditional burger condiments.

(SERVES 6, TWO SLIDERS PER SERVING)

Shredded Pork and Sauerkraut Sammies

Most of us have a love/hate affair with sauerkraut. My husband and I both grew up in the Midwest with the smells of baking pork and sauerkraut emanating from our German grandmothers' kitchens. He hated it! I loved it! I think the secret is that my grandmother thoroughly washed and drained the sauerkraut before cooking it with a bit of sugar.

1 tablespoon olive oil

1 (3 to 3½ pounds) pork loin roast

Salt

¼ teaspoon black pepper, plus more

1 cup chopped onions, like Vidalia

1 (32-ounce) bag sauerkraut, rinsed and drained

2 cups diced peeled apples

½ cup brown sugar

⅛ teaspoon ground cloves

12 sesame seed Kaiser buns

¾ cup cranberry or cherry honey mustard

12 slices Swiss cheese

At least 7 hours ahead: Place olive oil in a large non-stick skillet over medium heat. Season pork with salt and black pepper to taste. Sear all sides of pork in hot skillet until browned, about 3 minutes. Remove pork from skillet and set aside.

Place onions in skillet and sauté until softened, about 2 minutes. Transfer onions to a large bowl. Add sauerkraut, apples, brown sugar, ¼ teaspoon black pepper, and cloves to bowl. Toss to mix ingredients.

Place one-third of the sauerkraut mixture in the bottom of a slow cooker. Place seared pork roast on top. Spread remaining two-thirds sauerkraut mixture atop roast.

Cover and cook on low setting for 6 to 7 hours. Shred pork and mix it with sauerkraut. Season with salt and pepper to taste.

To serve: Preheat oven to 325 degrees F. Cut Kaiser buns in half, place on a baking sheet, and toast in oven. Spread ½ tablespoon cranberry mustard on the cut sides of each Kaiser bun. Place about ¾ cup shredded pork and sauerkraut mixture on bottom bun. Place 1 cheese slice atop pork. Replace top bun and cut sandwich in half.

(SERVES 12)

Korean Short Rib Bulgogi Tacos with Creamy Lime Vinaigrette

Bulgogi is a wildly popular Korean marinated beef barbecue. It is usually made with a tender cut of beef, such as ribeye or tenderloin, but it is more economical and even better with boneless short ribs.

FOR THE SHORT RIBS:

3 pounds boneless beef short ribs

1 cup soy sauce

½ cup dark brown sugar

⅓ cup mirin

¼ cup sesame oil

6 cloves garlic

6 scallions, cut into 1-inch pieces

2 teaspoons gingerroot paste

1 (8-count) package 6½-inch flour tortillas

1 (10.5-ounce) package chopped salad mix

Creamy lime vinaigrette

Sriracha (optional)

FOR THE CREAMY LIME VINAIGRETTE:

¼ cup fresh lime juice

3 tablespoons sour cream

2 teaspoons sugar

1 teaspoon garlic paste

½ teaspoon kosher salt

¼ teaspoon crushed red pepper flakes

¼ teaspoon ground cumin

At least one week ahead: To make the short ribs, cut off any excess fat from short ribs, then thinly slice the beef across the grain. Cut beef slices into 1½-inch pieces. Divide among three quart-size zipper bags.

In a blender, process soy sauce, dark brown sugar, mirin, sesame oil, garlic, scallions, and gingerroot until smooth. Pour one-third of the marinade into each zipper bag. Close bags and massage meat so that it is well coated with marinade. Freeze beef slices in the marinade until needed. (Each bag makes 8 tacos.)

To cook and serve: To make the creamy lime vinaigrette, whisk together lime juice, sour cream, sugar, garlic paste, kosher salt, red pepper flakes, and cumin. Place in a squeeze bottle or small cruet and refrigerate until needed.

Defrost 1 bag of beef and marinade. Heat a large sauté pan on high heat. Place short ribs and marinade in pan and cook for 3 to 4 minutes, tossing constantly, until beef is just cooked through.

Place 4 tortillas between two sheets of paper toweling. Microwave tortilla packet for 1 minute each. Repeat with remaining tortillas. (Heat only the number of tortillas you will need for each helping of tacos, so tortillas stay warm.)

To assemble tacos: Allow each diner to assemble their own tacos. Place a spoonful of the chopped salad mix in the middle of each tortilla. Drizzle it with creamy lime dressing. Place a spoonful of short rib meat atop slaw. Spoon a drizzle of pan sauce over meat. If desired, for additional kick, add a few drops of sriracha. Fold taco in half. Serve immediately.

Chef's note: Use only the chopped vegetables from the chopped salad mix. Save the dressing packet and garnishes for another time.

(MAKES 24 TACOS)

Smoked Salmon Egg Salad

A couple of tricks guarantee perfect hard-boiled eggs every time: Place eggs in a large saucepan covered by one inch of water. Don't crowd them or they may bump into one another. Bring water to boil over high heat. Cover pot and immediately remove it from heat. Allow eggs to sit in the hot water for ten minutes. Drain eggs, then rinse them with cold water. Place eggs in a bowl of ice water for a few minutes, which makes them easier to peel.

6 hard-boiled eggs, peeled and chopped

4 ounces smoked salmon, cut into small dice

½ cup minced red onions

2 tablespoons capers, rinsed and drained

2 tablespoons fresh dill

1 tablespoon fresh lemon juice

1 teaspoon grated fresh lemon peel

½ cup mayonnaise

Salt and freshly ground black pepper

At least 2 hours ahead: Mix eggs, salmon, onions, capers, dill, lemon juice, and grated lemon peel together in a medium bowl. Add mayonnaise and stir until ingredients are well coated and creamy. Add salt and pepper to taste. Transfer to a covered container and refrigerate until chilled.

Serve this gourmet egg salad between slices of bread for a sandwich, stuff it into toasted pita bread halves, or roll it with lettuce into a flour tortilla to form a wrap.

(MAKES 3 CUPS)

The Best of the Wurst

Up North, anytime two or more people get together, sausage is usually involved!

Wisconsin comes by its "sausage state" reputation quite naturally. Native American tribes made sausage of sorts, mixing the meat from deer and other game with wild rice, corn, fat, and/or berries. They then stuffed the mixture into animal skins or shaped it into patties and smoked them.

As settlers in the 1800s came to Wisconsin from Germany, Bohemia, and Poland, they brought their Old World recipes and sausage-making specialties. In later decades, other ethnic groups added to the sausage mix. Today, several large meat processors, such as Usinger's and Johnsonville, turn out multitudes of different sausage products, enjoyed nationwide, but many small, specialty meat markets remain, like Lake Tomahawk Meat Market, who still make their own specialty sausages.

If you're not from Wisconsin, you'll be forgiven if you think of sausage as the stuff atop your pizza or the breakfast link accompanying your eggs. You may have experienced kielbasa or maybe even our famous Wisconsin bratwurst (more on that later). But to really understand the depth and breadth of how sausage fits into the foodways here in Wisconsin, you'll need a primer to acquaint yourself with the types of sausage we produce here—cooked, dry and semi-dry, and fresh.

Cooked Sausage

Originating in Central Europe, **smoked sausage** is smoked and cured; no further cooking is needed. It is sold as links or ropes, has an edible casing, and has a robust smoky flavor.

Best known as kielbasa, **Polish sausage** is often named after the area or town where the recipe was developed. The key spices in this sausage are garlic and mustard seed.

Everyone knows the **frankfurter**, a.k.a. the hot dog, whose origins go back to thirteenth-century Germany. Originating in Germany and Italy, **ring bologna** is a long, tubular sausage formed in a ring shape. It is fully cooked, but it is often reheated. The casing should be removed before eating.

Dry and Semi-Dry Sausage

Kept without refrigeration, **summer sausage** is made from beef and/or pork and sometimes venison. Originating in Germany, it is often spiced with nutmeg, coriander, and mustard seed. **Snack sticks** are small, dried sausages, similar to salami and pepperoni. These sausages originated in the United States. Chewy and substantial, **landjaeger** is made into links of two and are sold in pairs. Prior to smoking, this regional favorite is pressed into a mold, giving them their signature look. The sausage originated in Germany, Austria, and Switzerland.

Fresh Sausage

Originating in Germany, **liverwurst** must contain at least 30 percent pork, beef, or veal liver. It comes in many flavors that vary by region, commonly marjoram and allspice. Most liverwurst is spreadable. **Italian sausage**, as we know it, originated in the United States, not in Italy. It is actually pork sausage seasoned with fennel or anise and, if the spicy variety, red pepper. Finally, the star wurst in the Wisconsin family, the **bratwurst**, originated in Bavaria. Usually made from pork, but sometimes also beef and veal, it is traditionally flavored with a mix of salt, pepper, nutmeg, and occasionally lemon, garlic, or sage. It is not unusual to find wildly different seasoning combinations—like cranberry, jalapeño, or cheddar—sold at small specialty meat markets, where they make their own. For instance, Louie's Finer Meats in Cumberland produces one hundred different kinds of bratwurst.

GETTY IMAGES

Wisconsin-Style Beer Bratwurst

Long considered the state's soul food, bratwurst, Wisconsin-style, sets the gold standard. Wisconsinites take their brats (pronounced "brot" not "braat") seriously and hold to a couple of hard and fast rules: Never boil bratwurst—lightly simmer them in beer and onions. Never serve a bratwurst on a hot dog bun; use a brat bun, which is slightly bigger. Never eat a bratwurst with a fork and knife. And never, ever put yellow mustard on a bratwurst—use a brown German-style mustard instead.

1 large sweet onion, like Vidalia

1 (5-count) package Original Flavor Johnsonville bratwurst

2 bottles beer

1 (5-count) package brat buns or hard rolls

Cut onion into thin slices. Set aside. Chop several slices to make 1 cup. Place chopped onions in a small, covered bowl and refrigerate until needed.

Place bratwurst in a large saucepan. Place sliced onions atop bratwurst. Pour beer over brats, so that they are submerged in liquid. If more liquid is needed, fill beer bottle with water and pour it into the pan. Simmer the brats on low for 10 minutes, until they plump up and have a milky-looking exterior. Do not bring to a boil.

Preheat an outdoor grill to hot. Using tongs, remove brats from pan; reserve beer-and-onion mixture. Place bratwurst on grill for 4 to 5 minutes, until underside is golden, without being burned. (Never pierce bratwurst with a fork; they will lose their juices.) Turn brats with tongs and cook 3 to 4 minutes longer, until underside is golden. (Don't allow the brats to split or get too black or they will dry out.)

Serve bratwurst immediately or return brats to the simmering beer-and-onion mixture (low heat) until ready to serve. (You can keep the wurst warm in the beer for up to 1 hour.) Toast buns briefly on grill rack before serving with cold chopped onions.

Brats are traditionally served with "the works," a choice of chopped onions, mustard, ketchup, and pickle relish. Purists believe adding sauerkraut is an abomination, but it remains a very popular condiment.

Chef's note: To do brats for a crowd, double or triple this recipe. Grill them ahead of time and serve them in a large pot of slightly simmering beer and onions. Keep extra brats warm in the beer mixture until people are ready for another. The simmering beer keeps the sausages moist.

(SERVES 5)

Mammatus clouds create a magic sky over Sand Island, one of Lake Superior's Apostle Islands.
GETTY IMAGES

Oodles of Noodles

Meatballs Four Ways

Make today meatball day! Mix up a batch of meatball base, divide it into four portions, spice each portion differently, roll and bake meatballs, then freeze them in freezer-weight zipper bags. Use the meatballs to create four distinctly different dishes: Greek Meatballs with Mediterranean Penne, Thai Meatballs in Red Curry Orzo, Hawaiian Meatballs in Sweet and Sour Sauce with Coconut Orzo, and Sicilian Meatballs in Fresh Tomato Sauce with Spaghetti (recipes on following pages).

Meatball Base

1 pound ground lamb

1 pound ground pork

2½ pounds ground beef (chuck)

2 cups chopped sweet onions, like Vidalia

2 cups Japanese panko breadcrumbs

2 teaspoons salt

½ teaspoon black pepper

4 large eggs

½ cup milk

2 teaspoons garlic paste or minced garlic

Up to 2 months ahead: Place lamb, pork, and ground beef in a large bowl. Add onions, breadcrumbs, salt, and pepper. Using clean hands, mix ingredients together until well combined.

Place eggs, milk, and garlic in a small bowl. Whisk together until blended. Pour egg mixture atop meat mixture. Mix ingredients together well with clean hands.

Divide meatball mixture equally among 4 medium bowls (about 1 pound, 7 ounces per bowl). Season meatball mixture in each bowl using the 4 recipes that follow.

(MAKES 18 MEATBALLS OF EACH VARIETY— 72 MEATBALLS TOTAL)

Greek Meatballs

½ cup feta cheese, crumbled

¼ cup chopped, seeded kalamata olives

¼ cup chopped roasted red bell peppers

2 teaspoons grated lemon zest

1 teaspoon Greek seasoning, like Penzey's

¼ of the meatball base mixture

- Add cheese, olives, roasted peppers, lemon zest, and Greek seasoning to meatball base mixture. Mix ingredients together well with clean hands.

Thai Meatballs

1 tablespoon grated orange zest

1 tablespoon Asian sweet chili sauce

1 teaspoon fish sauce

1 teaspoon gingerroot paste or minced gingerroot

2 tablespoons snipped fresh mint

¼ of the meatball base mixture

- Add orange zest, chili sauce, fish sauce, gingerroot, and mint to meatball base mixture. Mix ingredients together well with clean hands.

Hawaiian Meatballs

½ cup chopped water chestnuts

1 tablespoon soy sauce

2 teaspoons sesame oil

1 teaspoon gingerroot paste or minced gingerroot

½ teaspoon crushed red pepper flakes

¼ cup chopped sliced almonds

¼ of the meatball base mixture

- Add water chestnuts, soy sauce, oil, gingerroot, red pepper flakes, and almonds to meatball base mixture. Mix ingredients together well with clean hands.

Sicilian Meatballs

3 tablespoons snipped fresh, flat-leaf parsley

1½ teaspoons Italian seasoning, like Penzey's

½ cup grated Parmesan cheese

¼ cup pine nuts, dry toasted

¼ cup dried currants

¼ of the meatball base mixture

- Add parsley, Italian seasoning, Parmesan cheese, pine nuts, and currants to meatball base mixture. Mix ingredients together well with clean hands.

To make the meatballs: Preheat oven to 400 degrees F. Working with one type of meatball at a time, form meatball mixture into 2-inch balls. Place each in the cup of a mini-muffin pan. Bake for 15 minutes. Turn meatballs over in muffin cups and bake for 8 minutes longer. Repeat process until all meatballs have been baked. Remove meatballs from muffin cups and place each type on a separate dinner plate to cool.

To store meatballs: Place cooled meatballs in freezer-weight zipper bags by variety. Label and freeze until needed.

To serve meatballs: Use meatballs in the 4 recipes that follow.

Chef's note: The baking process moves along faster if you have several 18-count mini-muffin pans.

Greek Meatballs with Mediterranean-Sauced Penne

Kalamata olives, capers, tomatoes, and feta cheese marry in this no-cook sauce that goes together in minutes.

2½ cups chopped plum tomatoes (about 1 pound)

3 tablespoons minced, seeded kalamata olives

1 tablespoon capers, rinsed and drained

1 teaspoon garlic paste or minced garlic

¼ teaspoon salt

⅛ teaspoon crushed red pepper flakes

1 tablespoon red wine vinegar

1 tablespoon olive oil

2 tablespoons snipped fresh basil

½ pound penne pasta

18 frozen Greek meatballs, defrosted (page 61)

1 cup beef broth

½ cup crumbled tomato-basil feta cheese, divided

Early in the day: Make the sauce. Combine tomatoes, olives, capers, garlic, salt, crushed red pepper flakes, vinegar, olive oil, and basil in a medium bowl. Toss to mix well. Transfer to a covered container and refrigerate until needed.

To serve: Bring a large pot of water to boil over high heat. Add penne. Reduce heat to medium and cook to al dente, about 12 minutes, following manufacturer's instructions.

Meanwhile, remove Mediterranean Sauce from refrigerator and transfer to a large serving bowl. Allow sauce to come to room temperature. Place meatballs and beef broth in a large nonstick skillet over medium-low heat. Simmer for 10 minutes, until meatballs are heated through.

Drain penne and toss it with pasta sauce. Add ¼ cup feta cheese and toss to combine. Remove meatballs from broth with a slotted spoon and place in a serving bowl. Sprinkle remaining ¼ cup feta cheese over meatballs. Serve immediately.

Chef's note: Kalamata olives are oil-cured black olives often used in Mediterranean dishes. You can find them with conventional olives in your supermarket.

(SERVES 4)

Thai Meatballs in Red Curry Orzo

Defrosting the meatballs in the red curry sauce adds a little bit of water to the sauce, which thins it nicely upon reheating.

1 (14-ounce) can coconut milk

2 teaspoons red curry paste

2 tablespoons brown sugar

1 tablespoon fish sauce

1 tablespoon fresh lime juice

⅓ cup snipped fresh Thai basil

18 frozen Thai meatballs (page 61)

Orzo, for serving

Early in the day or the day before: Make the curry sauce. Heat coconut milk in a large nonstick saucepan over medium-low heat. Add red curry paste and stir until melted. Add brown sugar, fish sauce, and lime juice and stir until sugar is melted. Stir in basil. Simmer for 1 minute. Add frozen meatballs to curry sauce. Stir to combine. Transfer meatballs and sauce to a covered container and refrigerate until needed.

To serve: Place meatballs and red curry sauce in a large nonstick saucepan over low heat. Simmer for 10 minutes, stirring gently and turning meatballs, until meatballs and sauce are heated through. Serve atop hot orzo.

Chef's note: Prepare orzo while you are reheating meatballs and sauce: Bring salted water to boil in a medium saucepan. Stir in desired amount of orzo. Cook for 10 minutes or until orzo is al dente. Drain and serve.

(SERVES 4 TO 6)

Hawaiian Meatballs in Sweet and Sour Sauce with Coconut Orzo

This sweet and sour sauce reflects the multiple culinary cultures fused in the flavors of Hawaii.

18 frozen Hawaiian meatballs (page 61)

1 tablespoon olive oil

1 teaspoon garlic paste or finely minced garlic

1 teaspoon gingerroot paste or finely minced gingerroot

1 cup finely chopped onion

1 cup chopped red bell pepper

1 cup chopped green bell pepper

2 (8-ounce) cans pineapple chunks in own juice

2 cups chicken broth

3 tablespoons soy sauce

¼ cup cider vinegar

3 tablespoons brown sugar

2 tablespoons honey

½ teaspoon Chinese five spice seasoning

2 tablespoons cornstarch

¼ cup sweetened flaked coconut, dry toasted

¼ cup sliced almonds, dry toasted

Coconut orzo, for serving

Early in the day: Defrost meatballs. Place olive oil in a large nonstick skillet over medium heat. When oil is hot, add garlic, gingerroot, and onions. Sauté for 1 minute, stirring constantly. Add red and green bell peppers and sauté for 1 minute. Transfer onion mixture to a dinner plate.

Drain juice from pineapple chunks in a sieve, reserving juice. Cut each pineapple chunk in half and set aside. Transfer juice to skillet. Add broth, soy sauce, vinegar, brown sugar, honey, and five spice seasoning. Stir ingredients, increase heat to medium-high, and bring mixture to a boil. Reduce heat to low and simmer, uncovered, for 5 minutes.

Remove skillet from stove. Add onion mixture and pineapple. Transfer to a covered container and place in refrigerator, uncovered, to cool. When sauce is cool, cover container and refrigerate until needed.

To serve: Place sauce in a large nonstick saucepan over medium-low heat. Mix the cornstarch with 2 tablespoons sauce liquid. Stir cornstarch mixture into sauce. Add meatballs to sauce. Simmer on low heat for 15 minutes, until meatballs have heated through and sauce has thickened. (If sauce is too thin, mix 1 more tablespoon cornstarch with 1 tablespoon warm sauce liquid, stir into sauce, and simmer for several more minutes.) Place meatballs and sauce in a large shallow serving bowl. Mix coconut and almonds together in a small bowl. Serve meatballs and sauce atop coconut orzo (see "Chef's note" below). Sprinkle coconut-almond mixture atop each serving.

Chef's note: Prepare coconut orzo while you are reheating the meatballs and sauce. Combine 1 cup light coconut milk and 1½ cups water in a medium saucepan over medium heat. Bring mixture to a boil and add 1 cup orzo. Cook orzo for 10 minutes, until al dente. Drain and serve.

(SERVES 4 TO 6)

Sicilian Meatballs in Fresh Tomato Sauce with Spaghetti

Even the Godfather would love these classically Italian meatballs, which bask in a smooth, garlicky sauce made from fresh plum tomatoes.

2 tablespoons olive oil

1½ cups chopped sweet onions, like Vidalia

2 teaspoons minced garlic or garlic paste

5 cups (about 3 pounds) ripe plum tomatoes, peeled, seeded, and diced

1 teaspoon dried marjoram

2 teaspoons dried basil

1½ teaspoons salt

18 frozen Sicilian meatballs (page 61)

Spaghetti, for serving

Up to 2 weeks ahead: Make fresh tomato sauce. Heat olive oil in a large nonstick saucepan over medium heat. Add onions and sauté, stirring frequently, for 3 minutes. Add garlic, and sauté, stirring frequently, for 1 minute more. Add tomatoes and stir to mix well with onions. Cook for 15 minutes, stirring frequently.

Transfer tomato mixture to a blender and pulse until tomatoes are pureed. Wipe out saucepan and return tomato mixture to pan. Add marjoram, basil, and salt. Reduce heat to low, place saucepan on stove, and simmer, stirring frequently, for 10 minutes.

Transfer tomato sauce to a covered container. Place in refrigerator, uncovered, for 30 minutes, so that sauce can quickly cool. Cover container and refrigerate until needed (up to 3 days) or freeze (up to 1 month).

To serve: Defrost meatballs and tomato sauce. Place both in a large saucepan over medium-low heat. Reheat, stirring gently, until meatballs and sauce are heated through, 10 to 15 minutes. Place in a large serving bowl. Toss with spaghetti (see "Chef's note" below).

Chef's note: Prepare spaghetti while you are reheating meatballs and sauce. Bring a large pot of water to boil. Add 1 pound dried spaghetti and cook to al dente, following manufacturer's instructions, 10 to 12 minutes.

(SERVES 4 TO 6)

Italian Meatless Sauce

When tomato sauce simmers all day, packed with flavorful vegetables, herbs, and spices—that's Italian. Commonly referred to as "gravy" by Italian cooks in the old country, the sauce traditionally is made in large quantities and used with all kinds of pasta, as well as becoming the base for a myriad of dishes.

1 cup dried porcini mushrooms

1 tablespoon olive oil

2 cups chopped sweet onions, like Vidalia

1 cup finely chopped celery

2 teaspoons garlic paste or finely minced garlic

1 cup snipped fresh parsley

1 teaspoon snipped fresh rosemary

½ teaspoon dried sage leaves

1 (28-ounce) can San Marzano whole tomatoes (or other canned Roma tomatoes with juice), tomatoes chopped and juices reserved

1 (14.5-ounce) can Hunt's Fire Roasted diced tomatoes with garlic, juices reserved

4 (8-ounce) cans tomato sauce with basil, garlic, and oregano

1 small dried red chili pepper

1½ teaspoons salt

Place dried mushrooms in a small bowl. Add water until mushrooms are just covered. Set aside.

Meanwhile, place oil in a large nonstick skillet over medium heat. Add onions, celery, garlic, parsley, rosemary, and sage. Sauté for 5 minutes, stirring frequently. Transfer vegetables to a 4-quart slow cooker. Add chopped and diced tomatoes with their juices, tomato sauce, chili pepper, and salt. Stir to combine.

Remove mushrooms from soaking liquid with a slotted spoon. Chop mushrooms and add them to slow cooker. Add ¼ cup soaking liquid to slow cooker and stir until ingredients are well combined. Cover and cook on low setting for 8 to 9 hours.

Place sauce in a food mill and process in batches. Transfer to covered containers and refrigerate or freeze until needed.

Chef's note: If you don't have a food mill, you can puree sauce in a blender. The consistency will be slightly different but the taste will be the same.

(MAKES 8 CUPS)

Braciole

Southern Italians usually use bottom round for their long-braised braciole, an inventive dish that makes the most of a small amount of meat. In the United States, however, what is sold as "bottom round" or "beef for braciole" is not as marbled as its counterpart in Italy. Since a little marbling is prerequisite for tender braciole, look for any thinly cut steak streaked with fat when making this recipe.

1½ pounds thinly sliced New York strip steak (4 slices)

4 thin slices prosciutto

2 cloves garlic, finely minced

2 tablespoons pine nuts

2 tablespoons raisins

½ cup snipped fresh flat-leafed parsley

1¼ cups freshly grated Parmesan cheese, divided

Salt and freshly ground black pepper

2 cups Italian Meatless Sauce (page 67)

¾ pound penne pasta

½ cup grated Parmesan cheese

At least 4 hours ahead: Trim excess fat from edges of steak slices. Place each steak slice between 2 large sheets of waxed paper and pound with a mallet until steak is ¼-inch thick. Place 1 slice prosciutto atop each pounded steak slice. Sprinkle each steak with equal amounts of garlic, pine nuts, raisins, parsley, and ¾ cup Parmesan cheese. Add salt and pepper to taste. Roll up each slice like a sausage, tucking in the sides as you roll. Tie each rolled steak with kitchen string, crosswise and lengthwise.

Coat a 2-quart slow cooker with vegetable cooking spray. Place braciole rolls in slow cooker. Pour tomato sauce evenly atop rolls. Cover slow cooker and cook on low setting for 3 to 4 hours, until meat has cooked through and sauce is bubbly.

Bring a large pot of water to boil over high heat. Cook penne to al dente according to package directions, about 8 minutes. Drain pasta. Remove braciole from sauce and cut and remove strings. Toss drained penne and sauce together in a large bowl.

To serve: Divide sauced penne among four individual pasta bowls. Top each with a braciole. Sprinkle each serving with 2 tablespoons grated Parmesan cheese.

Chef's note: Some supermarkets sell thin cuts of steak, but to get really thin slices—round, chuck, skirt, strip, or flank—have a butcher cut them for you.

(SERVES 4)

Four-Cheese Macaroni and Cheese

Smoked Gouda is smoked in a brick oven over hickory chip embers. It has a slightly nuttier flavor than regular Gouda, and because it has 45 percent butterfat, it is buttery, smooth, and creamy.

2 cups small elbow macaroni

½ cup sour cream

3 large eggs

4 tablespoons butter, softened

½ teaspoon salt

½ teaspoon black pepper

1 cup heavy cream

½ cup grated Muenster cheese

½ cup grated smoked Gouda

½ cup grated provolone

½ cup grated sharp cheddar cheese

1 (3.5-ounce) package crispy fried onions

1 heaping tablespoon snipped fresh chives

Early in the day or up to 2 days ahead: Bring a large saucepan of salted water to a boil over high heat. Add macaroni and cook, stirring occasionally, until macaroni is al dente, 8 to 10 minutes or following package instructions.

While macaroni is cooking, whisk together sour cream, eggs, butter, salt, pepper, and heavy cream. Set aside until needed.

When macaroni is al dente, drain well and transfer it to a large bowl. Add all the cheeses, half the crispy fried onions, and chives. Add sour cream mixture to the bowl and stir to combine all ingredients well. Pour into a large, shallow baking dish that has been coated with olive oil cooking spray. Cover with cling wrap and refrigerate until needed.

To bake and serve: Preheat oven to 350 degrees F. Bring macaroni and cheese to room temperature. Remove cling wrap and bake for 30 to 45 minutes, until golden brown. Sprinkle remaining crispy fried onions atop macaroni and cheese and bake for 5 minutes more.

(SERVES 4 TO 6)

Sandhill cranes choreograph their flight. SHUTTERSTOCK

Savory Pies

Chicken Pot Pies

"Four and twenty blackbirds" are not baked in this pie, but chicken pot pie is thought to date back as far as the Middle Ages, where it was called a savory tart. Chefs in the royal kitchens of England and France considered the dish one of their most elaborate. This one is showy, too, but easy!

1 (15-ounce) jar whole cooked small onions

1 cup baby carrots, cut in quarters lengthwise

6 tablespoons butter

6 tablespoons flour

2 cups College Inn Chicken Bold Stock

½ cup heavy cream

½ cup half-and-half

½ teaspoon black pepper

¼ teaspoon salt

1 teaspoon dried marjoram

1 rotisserie chicken, cut in bite-size pieces (about 4 cups)

1 cup chopped celery

1 cup sliced fresh button mushrooms

¾ cup frozen peas, thawed

1 (10-ounce) package puff pastry shells

Early in the day or the day before: Drain onions and cut them in half. Set aside. Place carrots in a microwave-safe dish and microwave for 1 minute. Set aside.

Melt butter in a large saucepan over medium-low heat. Stir in flour, 1 tablespoon at a time. Stirring constantly, slowly add broth, cream, and half-and-half. Season the cream mixture with pepper, salt, and marjoram. Cook mixture, stirring constantly, until it is slightly thickened, about 1 minute.

Add chicken, celery, mushrooms, peas, onions, and carrots. Toss ingredients until well coated with sauce. Evenly divide chicken and vegetable mixture among six 1½-cup round ramekins. Cover with cling wrap and refrigerate until needed.

To bake: Preheat oven to 400 degrees F. Bring pot pies to room temperature. Place frozen puff pastry shells on a nonstick baking sheet. Place pot pies and pastry shells in oven and bake for 20 minutes, until mixture is bubbly and pastry is golden.

To serve: With a tablespoon, make a well in the middle of each pot pie. Place a pastry shell in each well. Serve immediately.

(SERVES 6)

Cottage Pies

This traditional English minced pie is called cottage pie when it is made with beef and shepherd's pie when it is made with lamb.

1 tablespoon olive oil

1½ cups chopped sweet onions, like Vidalia

½ cup chopped baby carrots

1 teaspoon garlic paste or finely minced garlic

1½ cups sliced button mushrooms

¼ teaspoon crushed red pepper flakes

¼ teaspoon dried thyme

Salt and freshly ground black pepper

1½ pounds ground beef

2 tablespoons flour

1 cup beef broth

1 (24-ounce) package Simply Potatoes Traditional Mashed Potatoes

Place oil in a large nonstick skillet over medium heat. Add onions, carrots, and garlic and sauté, stirring frequently, for 2 minutes. Add mushrooms, red pepper flakes, thyme, and ½ teaspoon salt, and sauté for 1 minute. Set aside.

Place ground beef in a medium nonstick skillet over medium heat. Cook beef, stirring occasionally, until meat is no longer pink. Drain meat in a colander and transfer to skillet with vegetable mixture. Stir to combine.

Place skillet over medium heat. Stir in flour. Slowly stir in beef broth and cook, stirring occasionally for 2 minutes, until thickened slightly. Divide beef mixture evenly among four 1½-cup ramekins. Cover with cling wrap and aluminum foil and refrigerate or freeze until needed.

Preheat oven to 375 degrees F. Bring cottage pies to room temperature. Microwave potatoes following manufacturer's instructions. Season potatoes with salt and pepper to taste. Top cottage pies with equal amounts of potatoes. Bake for 15 minutes, until potatoes are golden and pie is bubbly.

Chef's note: Add ½ cup shredded sharp cheddar cheese for an even cheesier potato topping. You can use any leftover mashed potatoes for this recipe.

(SERVES 4)

Mexican Burrito Pie

Like enjoying a taco, burrito, and enchilada all in one, this pie is a breeze to prepare and serve. As an added benefit, the recipe calls for ingredients you can keep on hand so it is a great choice when unexpected company rolls in. You can substitute taco mix for the burrito seasoning mix if you like.

2 pounds lean ground beef

1 large onion, finely chopped

1 yellow bell pepper, seeded and finely chopped

2 large cloves garlic, minced

1 (1½-ounce) package burrito seasoning mix

2 (8-ounce) cans roasted garlic tomato sauce

1 pound frozen baby gold and white corn, defrosted

1 cup sliced black olives (6-ounce can unsliced, pitted black olives)

1 (4-ounce) can mild, diced green chilies, drained

12 corn tortillas (20-ounce package)

8 ounces white sharp cheddar cheese, shredded

2 cups crumbled white corn tortilla chips

Sour cream, for serving

Fresh salsa, for serving

Up to two days ahead: Coat a large nonstick skillet with vegetable cooking spray. Place skillet over medium heat. Add ground beef and sauté, stirring frequently, until browned, about 10 minutes. Add onion, bell pepper, and garlic and cook until onion is soft, about 10 minutes more. Reduce heat to low. Add seasoning mix and stir until beef mixture is well coated. Add tomato sauce and stir to combine. Cover and simmer beef mixture 10 minutes, stirring occasionally.

Meanwhile, in a medium bowl, mix together corn, olives, and chilies. Set aside.

Coat a 9 x 13 x 3-inch baking dish with vegetable cooking spray. Cut 3 tortillas in half. Place tortilla halves in the bottom of the baking dish, cut sides abutting the edges of the dish. Place a whole tortilla in the spaces in the center of the dish.

Place half the meat mixture atop the tortilla layer. Then place half the corn mixture atop the meat and half the cheese atop the corn mixture. Repeat the four layers: tortillas, meat, corn, cheese. Cover baking dish with aluminum foil and refrigerate for up to two days.

To bake and serve, preheat oven to 375 degrees F. Bring burrito pie to room temperature. Top it with crumbled tortilla chips. Bake uncovered for 30 minutes. Remove from oven and allow to rest for 5 minutes. Serve pie with sour cream and salsa on the side.

(SERVES 8 TO 10)

Pork and Apple Pie

This recipe is a long way from the medieval English version that called for five pounds of lard, fourteen pounds of flour, and the trimmings of a butchered hog! But in fine British tradition, sage-seasoned pork and apples are encased in flaky pastry.

2 tablespoons olive oil, divided

2 pounds pork tenderloin, cut into ¾-inch pieces

1 large onion, sliced then quartered

6 ounces portobello mushrooms (2), black pith removed, halved and sliced ¼-inch thick

3 Granny Smith apples, peeled, cored, and thinly sliced

1 tablespoon fresh lemon juice

1½ teaspoons sage

1½ teaspoons salt

¼ teaspoon crushed red pepper flakes

1 tablespoon Dijon mustard

1¼ cups apple juice, heated

2 tablespoons butter

¼ cup flour

Dash cinnamon

1 tablespoon sugar

2 tablespoons snipped fresh flat-leafed parsley

1 rolled Pillsbury Pie Crust for 9-inch pie

1 large egg, beaten with 1 tablespoon water

Up to 1 month ahead: Place 1 tablespoon olive oil in a large nonstick skillet over medium heat. Add pork and sauté, stirring constantly, until meat is browned on all sides. With a slotted spoon, remove pork to a large bowl and set aside.

Wipe out skillet with paper toweling. Add remaining 1 tablespoon olive oil. Add onions and mushrooms to hot skillet and sauté until vegetables are soft and released liquid has evaporated, about 2 minutes. Add apples and sauté 1 minute more. Add vegetables and apples to pork and mix well. Add lemon juice, sage, salt, red pepper flakes, and mustard to pork mixture and stir to mix well.

Microwave apple juice on high for 1 minute. Melt butter in a small saucepan over medium heat. Whisk in flour, forming a roué. Slowly whisk in warm apple juice and cinnamon, until mixture is smooth and thickened slightly. Stir apple juice sauce into pork mixture until ingredients are well coated.

Coat a 10-inch deep-dish pie plate with vegetable cooking spray. Transfer pork mixture to the pie plate. Sprinkle with sugar, then parsley. Cover with cling wrap, then aluminum foil, and refrigerate for up to 24 hours or freeze until needed.

To bake and serve: Preheat oven to 350 degrees F. Allow pie crust to reach room temperature, then unroll it on a large sheet of parchment paper. Roll with a rolling pin until crust is large enough to cover deep-dish pie plate with a 1-inch overhang. Lift edges of parchment paper and invert crust atop pie. Crimp edges of crust and cut a 1-inch slit in the center of the crust. Brush crust and crimped edges with egg wash. Bake for 45 minutes or until crust is golden brown and pie is bubbling.

(SERVES 6)

Pizza Pot Pie

In 2 B.C.E., French bakers encased a lamprey in pastry and gave it to their king, a delicacy he very much enjoyed. So, this is not the first pie in history to hold a surprise under the crust! Using turkey sausage and part-skim cheeses reduces the fat content and greasiness of this savory dish—not to mention the guilt—and no flavor is lost in the transition. This is a great dish to keep on hand in the freezer.

1 (19½-ounce) package Italian sweet turkey sausage

1 (19½-ounce) package Italian hot turkey sausage

1 (25-ounce) jar spicy tomato pasta sauce

1½ cups part-skim ricotta cheese

⅓ cup grated Parmesan cheese

⅓ cup snipped fresh parsley

1 teaspoon dried oregano

1 teaspoon dried marjoram

1 teaspoon dried basil

2 large eggs

Freshly ground black pepper

2½ cups shredded mozzarella cheese

1 (10-ounce) package Pillsbury Pizza Crust

Two days or up to 1 month ahead: Remove casings from sausages and crumble meat. Sauté crumbled sausage in a large nonstick skillet over medium heat until cooked through and browned, about 10 minutes. Drain well in a sieve and transfer to a large bowl. Add spicy tomato sauce to sausage and mix well to combine. Set aside.

Place ricotta and Parmesan cheeses, parsley, oregano, marjoram, and basil in a medium bowl. Stir to mix. Place 1 egg in a small bowl and beat it lightly with a fork. Add egg to cheese mixture and stir to combine. Add pepper to taste. Set aside.

Coat a 10-inch-round deep-dish pie plate with vegetable cooking spray. Place half the sausage mixture evenly in bottom of pie plate. Dot half the cheese and egg mixture evenly over sausage mixture. Top with half the mozzarella cheese. Repeat layers with remaining ingredients. (At this stage, you can cover pizza pot pie with cling wrap and aluminum foil and refrigerate for up to two days or freeze for up to a month. Defrost thoroughly before baking.)

To bake and serve: Preheat oven to 350 degrees F. Remove cling wrap and foil from pie plate. Unroll pizza dough onto a large sheet of parchment paper and stretch it into a circle about 1 inch larger than the deep-dish pie plate. Transfer pizza dough to top of pizza pie, smoothing dough evenly and tucking excess dough inside the dish around sausage mixture.

Place 1 egg and 1 tablespoon water in a small bowl and beat together with a fork. Brush egg wash evenly over pizza crust. Bake for 40 to 45 minutes, or until top is golden brown. Remove pizza pot pie from oven and allow it to rest for 10 minutes before serving.

(SERVES 8)

Deep gorges and cascading waterfalls make Copper Gorge State Park special. BAYFIELD CHAMBER OF COMMERCE

The Main Events

Boozy Marinated Steaks on the Grill

Nothing is more comforting on a warm summer night than a thick, juicy steak on the grill. Tenderize sirloin steak in one of these boozy marinades. You won't need to serve filet mignon for your family or guests to think they are eating at a fancy steakhouse.

Mustard and Jack Daniel's Marinated Sirloin Steak

Jack Daniel's is a Tennessee whiskey first created by Jasper Newton "Jack" Daniel in 1875.

½ cup Vidalia onion mustard

¼ cup Jack Daniel's whiskey

½ cup plus 2 tablespoons packed dark brown sugar

2 teaspoons Worcestershire sauce

3 pounds sirloin steak, cut 1¼ inches thick

One day ahead: Mix mustard, whiskey, brown sugar, and Worcestershire sauce together in a small bowl. Place steak in a freezer-weight zipper bag. Pour marinade into bag. Close bag and massage bag until steak is totally covered with marinade. Refrigerate overnight.

To cook: Preheat grill to medium-hot (450 degrees F). Remove steak from marinade. Place marinade in a microwave-safe container and microwave for 1 minute. Grill steak, basting with marinade and turning once, until medium rare, 5 to 6 minutes per side.

Remove steak from grill. Cut slices on a slight angle, about ⅜ inch thick. Serve immediately.

Chef's note: Vidalia onion mustard can be found in gourmet-type food stores or can be ordered online. Substitute a mixture of ¼ cup finely minced sweet onions and ½-cup Dijon or whole-seed mustard if you can't find the more exotic version. You can substitute another bourbon whiskey if you don't have Jack Daniel's.

(SERVES 8)

DAIRY FARMERS OF WISCONSIN

Beer-Marinated Sirloin Steak

One of the best ways to tenderize sirloin steak is to marinate it in beer. Beer has alpha acids and tannins that help break down the fibers of the meat, rendering it more tender.

⅔ cup beer (ale)

⅓ cup olive oil

1 teaspoon salt

¼ teaspoon garlic powder

¼ teaspoon black pepper

2½ pounds top sirloin steak, cut 1½ inches thick

The day before: Whisk beer, oil, salt, garlic powder, and pepper together in a medium bowl. Place steak in a large freezer-weight zipper bag. Pour marinade over steak in bag. Zip bag, then place it inside another zipper bag and close. Shake bag so that marinade evenly coats steak. Refrigerate overnight.

Preheat grill. Remove bag of marinating steak from refrigerator and let it get to room temperature. Remove steak from marinade and place on hot grill. Cook for 5 to 6 minutes. Turn steak and grill for 5 to 6 more minutes, until steak is medium rare. Cut steak into ½-inch slices and serve immediately.

Chef's note: For best results, use a good Wisconsin craft ale in this marinade. You'll only need two-thirds of a cup, so you can drink the rest of the bottle!

(SERVES 6)

The Beer Up Here

Wisconsin has been brewing beer since the mid-1800s, before it even was a state. So much beer, in fact, that "beer" and "Wisconsin" are nearly synonymous. Wisconsin's early immigrant population came from regions of Europe with a long tradition of beer making and consumption. (The Brewing History Society states that from 1850 to 1900, more than a million immigrants settled in Wisconsin, nearly a quarter of them from Germany.) Wisconsin had an abundance of fresh water, ice, forests for cooperage, and fertile agricultural land for growing barley and hops.

The early rural breweries were small, often serving small local settlements. By the 1860s, Pabst, Miller, Schlitz, Blatz, Heileman, and Leinenkugel—all common names to Wisconsin beer enthusiasts over the ensuing decades—were all brewing beer. By 1878, Wisconsin was home to 226 breweries, and by 1914, brewing beer was Wisconsin's fifth-largest industry. With Prohibition came bootlegging and wildcat "near beer" breweries. After its repeal, beer making turned from small-batch breweries to larger-scale industrialized production.

From 1962 to 1982, Wisconsin led the nation in beer production, with the afore-mentioned breweries intensely competing for market share. Since the first commercial brewery was established in 1835, Wisconsin had more than 800 breweries open and saw nearly 650 breweries close. By 1985, there were only seven mega-breweries, and by 2010, only Miller (MillerCoors), of the initial big six, remained. (Miller bought Leinenkugel's in 1988.)

Today, Wisconsin has just over 200 breweries. The New Glarus Brewing Company, famously known for their "Spotted Cow" brew, markets their beer only in Wisconsin. Microbreweries are peppered throughout the state. Each one focuses on brewing a qual-ity, flavorful artisan product in small batches, rather than the focus on barrels sold as the big breweries of yesteryear did. Each is unique, seemingly competing to come up with the most colorful names for their brews.

Up North microbreweries include the Angry Minnow Brewing Company, which brews its craft beers in a brick building built by a lumber baron in 1889. "River Pig Pale Ale" and "Oaky's Oatmeal Stout" are local favorites. South Shore Brewery in Ashland makes all their beer with hops grown only in Wisconsin. "Ice Caves," "Children of the Gourd," and "Sacred Cow" are among their specialty beers.

Minocqua Brewing Company in Minocqua creates political-statement progressive beer, such as ",la" (a vice presidential stout), "Bernie Brew," and "Filibuster Ale." The Rocky Reef Brewing Company is a small-batch brewery in Woodruff, featuring "Musky Bite," "The Outhouse," and "Grandpa's Toasted!" Some Nerve Brewing Company in Man-itowish Waters creates such offerings as "Gobsmacked Oatmeal Stout," "Cream Abdul Jabbar" (a cream ale), and "One Weiss at a Time," a German wheat beer.

One of the most cleverly named craft beer selections comes from Tribute Brewery in Eagle River, where each beer is a tribute to folklore of their town and comes with a tale. For instance, "Barefoot Charlie IPA": "Barefoot Charlie Haase was a colorful character who went barefoot all year long. He built and ran a tavern/museum/restaurant just south of Land O' Lakes, which featured intricate woodworking, all done by Charlie himself. Much like Barefoot Charlie, our India Pale Ale is bold, creative, and leaves a lasting impression."

There's no lack of creativity in the words or the flavors of Up North's ever-growing craft beer industry as evidenced by the aforementioned creations. But as one retired brewery official is quoted as having once said: "Beer is ninety-seven percent water and three percent none of your damn business!" The secrets shall remain in Wisconsin.

Company Meatloaf with Cranberry Ketchup

Invest in a molded loaf pan to turn everyday meatloaf into a company meal. The Nordic Ware Fancy Bundt Loaf Pan has a nonstick interior finish and makes a great baking pan for breakfast breads as well. The cranberry ketchup elevates the flavor profile of this recipe.

3 pounds ground beef (90 percent lean)

½ cup finely chopped sweet onions, like Vidalia

¾ cup raisins

¼ cup dried parsley

¾ teaspoon dry mustard

1½ tablespoons Parmesan cheese

2¼ teaspoons dried oregano

1½ teaspoons salt

⅜ teaspoon white pepper

⅜ teaspoon ground coriander

1 tablespoon garlic paste or finely minced garlic

3 large eggs, beaten

3 cups Japanese panko breadcrumbs

½ cup pine nuts

5 tablespoons Cranberry Ketchup (page 99)

Preheat oven to 350 degrees F. Liberally coat a 10-cup loaf pan with vegetable cooking spray and set aside. Place beef, onions, raisins, parsley, dry mustard, Parmesan cheese, oregano, salt, white pepper, coriander, and garlic in a large bowl. With clean hands, mix ingredients together well. Using the same method, mix in eggs, then breadcrumbs and pine nuts. Transfer meatloaf mixture to the prepared loaf pan. Press mixture firmly into the pan, filling all crevices.

Bake meatloaf, uncovered, for 1 hour. Spread cranberry ketchup atop meatloaf. Return meatloaf to oven and bake 15 minutes more. Gently remove meatloaf from the pan with two firm spatulas and place on a serving platter. (If using a decorative pan, up-end it on a serving platter.) Slice and serve with additional cranberry ketchup on the side.

(SERVES 10 TO 12)

Hoisin–Ale Braised Short Ribs

Short ribs should be cooked "low and slow." The braising breaks down the connective tissue of the otherwise tough meat and renders it mouthwateringly tender. Ale, the oldest form of beer, is fruitier and more full-bodied than lager. Ales come in many forms. I used pale ale in this recipe.

4 to 4½ pounds beef short ribs

Salt and freshly ground black pepper

1 tablespoon olive oil

1 head garlic (12 to 15 cloves), cloves peeled and crushed

1½-inch piece of gingerroot, peeled and sliced ¼-inch thick

1 (12-ounce) bottle ale beer

3 tablespoons rice wine vinegar

¾ cup bottled hoisin sauce

Season all sides of ribs liberally with salt and pepper. Place oil in a large nonstick skillet over medium heat. Working in 2 batches, sear ribs on all sides. Transfer seared ribs to a 5-quart slow cooker.

Pour off all but 1 tablespoon fat and drippings. Add garlic and gingerroot and sauté, stirring constantly, for about 2 minutes. Transfer garlic and gingerroot to slow cooker with a slotted spoon.

Add ale and vinegar to slow cooker. Cook on low setting for 4½ to 5 hours, until meat is tender and pulling away from the bone. Remove ribs from slow cooker. Cut away meat from bone, removing any visible gristle.

Pour broth through a strainer into a large bowl. Return broth to slow cooker. Stir in hoisin sauce. Return boneless ribs to slow cooker. Cover and reduce heat setting to warm. Hold on warm for at least 30 minutes or up to 2 hours. Transfer short ribs to a serving platter. Season with salt and pepper to taste. Transfer sauce to a medium pitcher or bowl. Serve short ribs drizzled with sauce.

(SERVES 4)

Red Currant Glazed Corned Beef with Horseradish Cream

Before the days of refrigeration, beef was cured in salt brine for preservation. The term corned *refers to the corns, or grains, of salt in which it is cured.*

½ cup brown sugar, divided

1 teaspoon dry mustard

½ teaspoon black pepper

½ teaspoon ground cloves

1 4-pound flat-cut corned beef, rinsed and dried

1 tablespoon cider vinegar

1 tablespoon mint sauce or 2 sprigs fresh mint leaves

2 cups apple juice

1 (12-ounce) jar red currant jelly (1 cup)

¼ cup Dijon mustard

½ cup heavy whipping cream

3 tablespoons prepared horseradish

Early in the day: Mix 2 tablespoons brown sugar, dry mustard, pepper, and cloves together in a small bowl. Rub mixture into both sides of corned beef. Place corned beef in a slow cooker.

Mix 2 tablespoons brown sugar, vinegar, mint sauce, and apple juice in a medium bowl. Pour mixture over corned beef. Add water so that corned beef is just barely covered. Cook on high for 1 hour. Reduce heat to low and cook in slow cooker for 8 hours.

Preheat oven to 350 degrees F and coat a shallow baking pan with vegetable cooking spray. Remove corned beef from slow cooker, discarding liquid, and place in the prepared pan. Whisk remaining ¼ cup brown sugar, red currant jelly, and mustard together in a medium bowl. Pour glaze mixture over corned beef. Bake, uncovered, for 30 minutes. Spoon glaze (pooled in bottom of pan) atop corned beef. Bake for 15 minutes more.

Meanwhile, make the horseradish cream. Whip cream until soft peaks form, then fold in horseradish. Refrigerate until needed.

To serve: Slice corned beef across grain into ½-inch slices. Transfer remaining glaze into a small pitcher. Serve as sauce with the corned beef, accompanied by the horseradish cream.

Chef's note: If you don't want to cook corned beef in a slow cooker, place corned beef and cooking liquids in a large pot over high heat. Bring to a boil. Reduce heat to low, cover, and simmer for 3 hours, until tender. Then proceed with glazing and baking instructions, above.

(SERVES 8)

Smothered Cube Steaks

Cube steak is top round steak that has been tenderized and flattened in a meat-cubing machine. Its name refers to the indentations in the meat that that the tenderizing process creates. My mother always called cube steaks "minute steaks," and with good reason. It only takes about a minute per side to cook them. Smothered in caramelized onions and mushrooms, the steaks make a quick, tasty meal.

¾ pound cube steaks (about 3)

Salt and freshly ground black pepper

2 tablespoons butter, divided

1 large sweet onion, like Vidalia, halved and sliced

8 ounces button mushrooms, sliced

Season cube steaks generously with salt and pepper. Melt 1 tablespoon butter in a large skillet over medium-high heat. Add onion and cook, stirring frequently, until translucent, 5 to 6 minutes. Add mushrooms and cook, stirring frequently, until mushrooms are just cooked through and onions are caramelized, about 3 minutes more.

Remove onions and mushrooms to a plate and set aside. Add remaining 1 tablespoon butter to skillet. When butter has melted, add cube steaks and cook for 1 minute per side. Add onions and mushrooms to skillet, atop cube steaks, and cook for 30 seconds longer. Serve cube steaks immediately, smothered with onions and mushrooms.

(SERVES 2)

Wisconsin Cranberries

The humble cranberry, which makes its annual debut around Thanksgiving, is Wisconsin's official state fruit, and with good reason! Wisconsin is the country's leading producer of cranberries—more than 4 million barrels in 2021. (Each barrel holds 100 pounds, the industry standard.) The 21,000 acres of sand and peat marshes in central and northern Wisconsin provide the perfect growing conditions for cranberries.

Once called "crane berry" by early settlers in the state because its blossom resembled a sandhill crane, the cranberry was first harvested by settlers in Wisconsin in the 1830s, although undoubtedly the fruit was gathered even before that by the indigenous tribes before them. Today there are more than 250 growers in the state.

Cranberries are perennial plants that grow on low running vines in sandy and peaty bogs and marshes. At harvest, the cranberry beds are flooded with up to eighteen inches of water. The harvest method depends upon how the berries will be used. A picking machine harvests fruit that will be sold as fresh. The machines have tines that pass through the vines, knocking the berries off the vines and catching them, then sending them on a conveyor into a bin. Later, the fruit dries off in boxes with slatted bottoms and is stored in refrigerated buildings, where they are sorted and packaged for sale.

Fruit that will be processed into sauce, juice, sweetened dried fruit, or other products is wet harvested. A machine with a circular front beater is driven through the beds, loosening the fruit from the vines and knocking the berries into the water. The berries float

The cranberry bog is harvested with a berry pump in the fall. GETTY IMAGES

to the surface, where they are pushed into one corner and pumped out to the bed of a truck. (The berries contain a pocket of air, which makes them float in water.) Delivered to a processing station, they are cleaned, graded, and frozen. Only 5 percent of Wisconsin's cranberry harvest is sold as fresh berries.

Cranberries are harvested each year from late September through October. Up North cranberry farms are mainly around Manitowish Waters, Eagle River, Spooner, and Hayward. Two are open to the public during harvest season for tours: Lake Nokomis Cranberries in Eagle River (lakenokomiscranberries.com) and Manitowish Waters Cranberry Marsh Tours, in Manitowish Waters (manitowishwaters.org).

Cranberry Ketchup

Cranberries are among the fruits highest in antioxidants, which help memory function and coordination. This ketchup is great on a turkey sandwich, grilled chicken, even grilled cheese or with vegetables. But it's especially special in Company Meatloaf with Cranberry Ketchup (page 94).

1 (12-ounce) bag fresh cranberries, washed and picked through

1 cup white wine vinegar

3 cups chopped sweet onions, like Vidalia

2 teaspoons garlic paste or finely minced garlic

¾ cup sugar

1 tablespoon allspice

1 teaspoon salt

⅔ cup water

Place cranberries, vinegar, onions, garlic, sugar, allspice, salt, and water in a large nonstick saucepan over medium-low heat. Bring to a simmer and cook, stirring frequently, for 20 minutes, until very thick. Remove from heat and cool for 15 minutes.

Transfer cranberry mixture to a blender and puree until smooth. Pour ketchup into glass jars and refrigerate for up to 2 months.

Chef's note: Fresh cranberries are available in supermarkets only in the fall. When they are in season, pick up a couple of extra bags and store them in your freezer. They'll freeze well for up to one year. Do not thaw the frozen berries when you are ready to use them. Simply use frozen cranberries in place of fresh ones called for in your recipes.

(MAKES 2½ CUPS)

Sauerbraten

One of the national dishes of Germany, sauerbraten, or "sour roast," requires two steps in its preparation: marinating for at least two to three days, then slow cooking for six to eight hours. German settlers brought many versions of this braised pot roast to Wisconsin. Some used pork or buffalo meat, but beef rump roast is traditional.

1 (4-pound) rump roast

5 cups halved and sliced sweet onions, like Vidalia, divided

1 stalk celery, chopped

1 large carrot, peeled and chopped

2 bay leaves

4 whole cloves

6 black peppercorns

6 whole allspice seeds

½ teaspoon mustard seeds

½ teaspoon dried thyme leaves

1 cup red wine

1 cup red wine vinegar

2 cups water

1 teaspoon salt

½ teaspoon ground black pepper

3 slices bacon, cut into ½-inch strips

1 cup crushed gingersnaps

⅓ cup raisins

1 tablespoon molasses

Two to 3 days ahead: Place rump roast in a large freezer-weight zipper bag. Add 3 cups onions, celery, carrots, bay leaves, and cloves to bag. Place peppercorns and allspice in a mortar and crush with a pestle or place spices on a cutting board and crush them by pressing down hard on the side of a large knife blade. Place them in a small bowl. Add mustard seeds and thyme and stir to combine. Sprinkle spices over roast in bag. Mix wine, vinegar, and water together in a 4-cup measuring cup. Pour over roast. Close zipper on bag. Place zipped bag inside another freezer-weight zipper bag and massage until marinade ingredients are well mixed and covering roast. Refrigerate until needed, massaging bag several times each day.

To cook: Remove roast from marinade. Place on a cutting board and pat dry with paper toweling. Pour marinade through a strainer into a large measuring cup, discarding vegetables and spices and saving marinade. Sprinkle all sides of roast with salt and teaspoon pepper.

Place a large nonstick skillet over medium heat. Add bacon and cook until crispy, about 3 minutes. Remove bacon with a slotted spoon and drain on paper toweling. Add roast to skillet and brown on all sides. Place browned roast in a 4-quart slow cooker. Top with bacon and remaining 2 cups onions. Place 1 cup marinade in a microwave-safe container and microwave it for 1 minute. Pour marinade over roast. Cover slow cooker and cook for 6 to 8 hours, until meat is tender when tested with a knife, but not shredding.

Remove roast from cooking liquid and place on a cutting board. Wrap tightly with aluminum foil. Turn slow cooker up to high setting. Add gingersnaps, raisins, and molasses. Cover and cook for 10 minutes, until sauce has thickened. Cut roast into thick slices and place on a serving platter. Spoon sauce over sauerbraten and season with salt and pepper to taste. Serve remaining sauce on the side.

Chef's note: Serve with potato dumplings, potato pancakes, boiled new potatoes, spaetzle, or red cabbage. The crushed gingersnaps thicken the liquid of the sauce.

(SERVES 6 TO 8)

Wava's Family Favorite Pot Roast

My oldest and dearest friend, Wava, is a terrific cook. We grew up together in northern Wisconsin. Generations of her family have made this amazing pot roast. A simple recipe, it raises pot roast to a whole other level!

1 (3- to 4-pound) chuck roast

Salt and freshly ground black pepper

1 large onion, cut into 4 thick slices

2 to 3 bouillon cubes

1-pound bag carrots, scrubbed, peeled, and cut in half

6 to 8 medium Yukon Gold potatoes, peeled

Horseradish sauce, for serving

Preheat oven to 250 degrees F. Spray a 16-inch roasting pan with olive oil spray Place roast in pan. Season generously with salt and pepper. Place onion slices on top of chuck roast. Add ¼-inch water and bouillon cubes to pan. Cover pan tightly with aluminum foil and roast for 6 hours.

Remove roast from pan, place it on a platter, and cover it with aluminum foil. Increase oven temperature to 350 degrees F. Add carrots and potatoes to pan. Roll them around in the pan juices so all sides have been coated. Re-cover pan with foil and bake for 45 minutes to 1 hour. Check vegetables for doneness. Increase oven temperature to 400 degrees F. Add roast back to the pan. Continue baking, uncovered, until carrots and potatoes are nicely browned and roast has warmed through, about 30 minutes. Season vegetables with salt and pepper to taste. Cut pot roast into chunks with a fork and knife. (Meat will be so tender, it will fall apart.) Serve with horseradish sauce.

(SERVES 4 TO 6)

Brown Sugar Pork Loin Roast

Reminiscent of slow-roasted pork served on a Caribbean island with the background music of steel drums, this sweet and spicy dish welcomes an accompanying tray of icy margaritas.

2 teaspoons salt

½ teaspoon black pepper

1 teaspoon ground cumin

1 teaspoon chili powder

1 teaspoon cinnamon

2½- to 3-pound pork loin roast

2 tablespoons olive oil

1 packed cup dark brown sugar

2 tablespoons garlic paste or finely minced garlic

1 tablespoon Louisiana hot sauce or other favorite hot sauce

Five hours ahead: Mix together salt, pepper, cumin, chili powder, and cinnamon in a small bowl. Sprinkle seasoning mixture over all sides of pork and rub it into meat.

Place oil in a large nonstick skillet over medium heat. When oil is hot, add pork and sear on all sides and ends, about 30 seconds per side. Transfer to a 4-quart slow cooker.

Mix brown sugar, garlic, and hot sauce together in a medium bowl to form a paste. Spread the paste over the entire top of the pork roast. Cover slow cooker and cook on low setting for 4 hours. Open slow cooker and turn roast over with a sturdy fork. Re-cover slow cooker and cook for 1 hour more, until pork is cooked through and tender but not shredding. Slice pork and drizzle with brown sugar sauce. Serve remaining sauce on the side.

Chef's note: The government guideline for freshness dating of spices is four years for whole spices and two years for ground spices. It is believed the flavor of the spices begins to dissipate over time. If you are unsure how old your spices are, smell them. If they smell spicy and strong, keep them. If not, either replace them or simply use a larger amount in your dish.

(SERVES 4 TO 6)

Blackberry-Glazed Pork Tenderloin

Roast tenderloins to an internal temperature of 150 degrees F for medium (warm, pink center), which is above the 137 degrees F necessary to kill any trichinae. Be careful not to overcook pork tenderloin, one of the leanest meats you can eat. Tenderloins are more expensive than other cuts, but they cut like butter and melt in your mouth.

½ cup blackberry preserves

3 tablespoons water

2 tablespoons Worcestershire sauce

2 tablespoons cider vinegar

1 tablespoon sweet chili sauce

1 (2½-pound) package pork tenderloins

2 large cloves garlic, sliced lengthwise

2 tablespoons olive oil, divided

1 teaspoon fresh rosemary

½ teaspoon kosher salt

¼ teaspoon cracked black pepper

½ pint fresh blackberries (optional)

Preheat oven to 425 degrees F. Place preserves, water, Worcestershire sauce, vinegar, and chili sauce in a small saucepan over medium heat. Cook sauce, stirring occasionally, until preserves are melted, about 2 minutes. Remove from heat and cover.

Make 4 slits in the tenderloins, several inches apart. Place garlic slices in slits. Brush top of tenderloins with 1 tablespoon oil. Sprinkle rosemary atop tenderloins. Season with salt and pepper.

Heat remaining 1 tablespoon oil in a large skillet over medium-high heat. Sear the tenderloins until browned on all sides, about 3 minutes in total. Remove tenderloins from skillet and place in a foil-lined baking pan. Baste with blackberry sauce.

Place tenderloins in oven for 8 minutes. Baste with sauce and return to oven for 7 more minutes. Remove tenderloins from oven and tent with aluminum foil. Allow tenderloins to rest for 5 minutes. Cut into ½-inch slices on the diagonal. Place on a serving platter. Drizzle with blackberry sauce. Sprinkle tenderloin with blackberries if desired. Serve with remaining sauce.

(SERVES 6)

Orange-Mustard Glazed Baked Ham with Horseradish Cream Sauce

Located in the Chippewa Valley, Wisconsin's Huntsinger Farms is the world's largest grower and processor of horseradish, which they market under the familiar Silver Spring label. (It is the number-one retail brand in the United States.) Family owned and operated for four generations, the operation now encompasses more than 7,000 acres.

1 (8- to 9-pound) spiral ham

½ cup Triple Sec liqueur

2 tablespoons cranberry honey mustard

½ cup orange juice

1 tablespoon grated orange peel

⅛ teaspoon plus a pinch ground nutmeg

¼ cup honey

1 teaspoon cracked black pepper, plus more

1 teaspoon coarse salt, plus more

½ cup heavy whipping cream

1 heaping tablespoon prepared horseradish

1 teaspoon white balsamic vinegar

Preheat oven to 350 degrees F. Coat a shallow baking pan with vegetable cooking spray. Place ham, cut-side down, in pan. Cover with aluminum foil. Bake for 45 minutes.

Meanwhile, place liqueur, mustard, orange juice, orange peel, nutmeg, honey, cracked pepper, and coarse salt in a small saucepan over medium heat. Bring to a boil, stirring frequently. Reduce heat to low and simmer, stirring occasionally, for 5 minutes.

In the bowl of an electric mixer, beat whipping cream until thick but not stiff, about 2 minutes. With mixer on low speed, fold in horseradish, vinegar, and salt and pepper to taste. Transfer to a small serving bowl and refrigerate until needed.

Remove foil from ham. Pour one-third of the orange-mustard glaze over ham. Bake for 10 minutes. Pour another one-third of glaze over ham. Bake for 10 minutes. Pour final one-third glaze over ham and bake for 10 minutes more.

Remove ham from pan, cut spiral pieces away from the bone, and place on a serving platter. Transfer any remaining glaze in the pan into a small serving bowl. Serve orange-mustard glaze and horseradish cream sauce as enhancements with the ham.

(SERVES 12 TO 16)

What's a Hodag, and What Is It Doing in Rhinelander?

Scotland may have their Loch Ness Monster, but here Up North, the Hodag commands mythological precedence. Long the subject of lumber-camp tall tales about a monster that roamed the local forests for more than a century, the Hodag wasn't just any ordinary beast.

In 1893, Eugene Simeon Shepard claimed he came face-to-face with a Hodag while hiking near his Rhinelander home. Shepard described it as a 185-pound, 7-foot-long, lizard-like beast with a disproportionately large horned head, long fangs, and green eyes. Four short, sturdy legs rose from its clawed feet, supporting a stout, muscular body, the back of which was covered with spikes. Shepard regaled that the beast emitted smoke and fire from its nostrils, which smelled like "a combination of buzzard meat and skunk perfume." Shepard claimed he ran for his life.

Shepard, a bit of a prankster, wouldn't let go of the story. He claimed to have organized hunting parties to capture the Hodag. In the fall of 1896, he returned from such a hunting trip regaling that he and a group of lumberjacks had captured the mythical beast in his den, asphyxiating it with chloroform. Shepard purportedly transported the Hodag to a pit in a dimly lit tent at the Rhinelander Fairgrounds, merely days before the opening of the Oneida County Fair, a rather curious coincidence. Here, for a fee, Shepard

Rhinelander's famed mascot—Hodag—"guards" the Chamber of Commerce.
RHINELANDER CHAMBER OF COMMERCE

displayed the snarling, growling Hodag in his "den" hidden behind a curtain, at a distance from onlookers.

Shepard's Hodag caused such a stir, he began touring county fairs around northern Wisconsin and finally "displayed" the beast in a barn at his home in Rhinelander, attracting thousands of curious paying visitors over the years. Shepard put on quite a show. He would go behind the curtain and approach the Hodag, whose shadow could be seen. A commotion appeared to ensue, with snarling, growling, ripping, snapping, and breaking sounds coming from behind the curtain. Shepard would reappear to the audience with his clothes in tatters and inform the audience that the Hodag was too angry to be seen that day.

Newspapers around the country heralded Shepard's Hodag as an authentic scientific discovery, prompting a group from the Smithsonian Institution to plan a trip to Rhinelander in 1900 to investigate. Realizing the jig was up, Shepard came clean and admitted the Hodag was all an elaborate hoax. Shepard and his friend Luke Kearney had constructed the Hodag from a large stump, covered it in with oxen hide, and added horns and spikes taken from dead oxen and cattle. They controlled the beast's movements with wires. The Hodag's growl and snarl were provided by Shepard's sons, who hid themselves away in the Hodag den.

The confession did nothing to dim the Hodag's popularity. Thousands of people continued to come to Rhinelander to view Shepard's creation and, in doing so, discovered the pristine beauty of the area. (There are 232 lakes within 15 minutes of downtown Rhinelander, thousands of acres of public forest, and 1,000 miles of snowmobile trails.) Shepard's original Hodag was destroyed by fire early in the twentieth century.

Over the years the Hodag became the city's legendary mascot—a mysterious, ferocious, mischievous creature, the official symbol of Rhinelander—Hodag City. A small Hodag was presented to Senator John F. Kennedy and Mrs. Kennedy in 1959 when they visited Rhinelander for his presidential campaign. Every year for four days in July, Rhinelander hosts the Hodag Country Festival, which features performances by the biggest names in country music.

Hodag Tales

- "In the 1890s the Hodag ate mud turtles and water snakes, oxen and white bulldogs, but only on Sundays!"
- "The Hodag snatched fish right off the line but preferred a traditional Northwoods Friday night fish fry with potato pancakes!"
- "The Hodag's horns were magic. When powdered and consumed, it would make a person immune to the effects of alcohol and be able to go without sleep for seven days and seven nights!"

Hodag Brisket

Okay, so it's not really made with Hodag, but it's a tasty, deceptively simple hoax.

1 (4- to 4½-pound) beef brisket

1 tablespoon olive oil

1 (14-ounce) can cranberry sauce

½ cup orange juice

1 (1-ounce) envelope Lipton onion soup mix

Cut brisket in half, crosswise, into 2 similarly sized pieces. Place oil in a large nonstick skillet over medium heat. When oil is hot, sear both sides of each brisket, about 30 seconds per side. Transfer brisket pieces to a dinner plate.

Mix cranberry sauce, orange juice, and onion soup mix together in a medium bowl. Place 1 piece of brisket in a 5- to 5½-quart slow cooker. Spoon half the cranberry mixture over brisket. Place remaining piece of brisket atop the other. Spoon remaining cranberry mixture over brisket.

Cover slow cooker and cook on low setting for 5 hours. Remove meat to a cutting board. Slice brisket against the grain into ¼-inch slices. Return brisket slices to slow cooker, making sure they are covered with sauce. Re-cover slow cooker and cook on low setting for 2 hours more, until meat is fork tender but not shredding.

Chef's note: The brisket is great served with roasted potatoes, onions, and carrots. Simply toss 2 cups of each, cut into 1½-inch pieces, with 1 tablespoon olive oil. Place on a nonstick baking sheet in a 350 degree F oven for the final hour the brisket is cooking.

(SERVES 8)

Spicy Minted Thai-Marinated Grilled Pork Chops

Fish sauce is a fermented liquid condiment that is commonly used in Southeast Asian cuisine. It tastes a little fishy and salty, but when paired with lime juice it achieves a tangy flavor balance.

½ cup fresh lime juice

3 tablespoons brown sugar

1½ tablespoons Thai fish sauce

1 tablespoon minced chili peppers

½ teaspoon minced garlic

⅓ cup snipped fresh mint

4 to 6 (1½-inch-thick) bone-in pork chops

Salt and freshly ground black pepper

Up to one day ahead: In a small saucepan over medium heat, combine lime juice, brown sugar, fish sauce, chili peppers, garlic, and mint. Bring to a boil, stirring occasionally. Boil 1 minute. Cool and refrigerate in a covered container until needed.

At least 4 hours ahead: Place pork chops in a shallow baking dish. Pour marinade over pork chops. Lift each chop slightly with a fork so that excess marinade flows underneath. Replace chops. Cover with cling wrap and refrigerate for 4 hours, turning chops every hour.

To cook and serve: Preheat gas grill to medium-high. Remove pork chops from marinade. Season with salt and pepper. Grill pork chops, basting with marinade occasionally, until just cooked through and still slightly pink, about 5 minutes per side. Microwave remaining marinade. Serve pork chops drizzled with warm marinade.

(SERVES 4 TO 6)

Grilled Rack of Lamb

A rack of lamb is the un-split primal rib of the lamb. Frenching means that the rack is cut so that the ribs are exposed. Silver skin must be removed because it is a connective tissue that does not break down during cooking. It would be chewy, tasteless, and undesirable.

1 (1¼- to 2-pound) Frenched rack of lamb

Dijon mustard

Olive oil spray

Penzey's Bavarian mix or another similar seasoning blend (see Chef's note below.)

Salt and freshly ground black pepper

Mint sauce or jelly, for serving (optional)

At least 1 hour ahead: Trim fat and silver skin from lamb. Spread Dijon mustard on both sides of lamb. Spray with olive oil. Sprinkle with seasoning blend. Put foil caps on the ends of the Frenched rack bones. Refrigerate rack of lamb for at least 1 hour.

Heat a gas grill with the searing burner on high and the other burner on low. Overall temperature should be 300 degrees F. Bring rack of lamb to room temperature for 15 minutes. Salt and pepper the meat. Cook lamb using the indirect method. Sear rack of lamb 2 minutes per side on the hot searing burner, then place rack on the low heat burner, bone side down, until internal temperature reads 120 degrees F, about 10 minutes. Remove meat and allow it to rest until the internal temperature reaches 130 degrees F, 5 to 10 minutes. Cut lamb between the ribs and divide between two dinner plates. Serve with mint sauce or mint jelly if desired.

Chef's note: You can order Bavarian seasoning at penzeys.com. It is a salt-free blend of crushed brown mustard seeds, rosemary, garlic, thyme, bay leaves, and sage. You can substitute another brand of similar seasoning if you wish.

(SERVES 2)

Beer Can Chicken

Yet another way to use Wisconsin beer! These little birds stand up proud on the grill, thanks to an ingenious, inexpensive little rack called a ChickCan. You can find the racks in the grilling section of most hardware and home improvement stores.

2 (4-pound) fryer chickens

Olive oil

2 (12-ounce) cans of your favorite beer

2 tablespoons Penzey's Singapore Seasoning or another seasoned poultry rub

Preheat gas grill to 350 to 400 degrees F. Place a shallow foil pan under the area upon which the chickens will cook, using gas burners in indirect method (burner off under chickens). Add a few hickory chips to the coals, if desired.

Rinse chickens thoroughly and dry with paper toweling. Coat chickens with olive oil spray or brush with olive oil. Rub seasoning all over the skin of both chickens. Set aside on a large tray.

Drink one-third of the beer out of each can (I'm not kidding! But you can pour it down the drain if you want.) Place each can of beer into a ChickCan rack and place the racks on the grill. Place the cavity of each chicken atop rack and beer can, so that chickens are "standing up." (The beer bubbles up in the heat, basting the chickens from within.) Grill chickens, covered, for 1¼ to 1½ hours, until chickens are golden brown. Remove chickens from racks and place on a tray. Allow them to rest for 5 to 10 minutes. Slice and serve immediately.

Chef's note: Penzey's spice company, based in Milwaukee, Wisconsin, concocts a number of wonderful rubs for meat, poultry, and fish that are packaged in small, affordable plastic jars. You can order online at www.penzeys.com.

(SERVES 8)

Cookout Kabobs

For people of the Middle East, Africa, Central and South Asia, as well as countries bordering the Mediterranean Sea, kabobs constitute pure comfort food. Consisting of grilled or broiled meats on a skewer or stick, kabobs have made their way around the world and rank high on the must-eat-at-a-summer-cookout for folks in America as well.

DAIRY FARMERS OF WISCONSIN

Yogurt-Onion Chicken Kabobs

The blanketing pita breads keep the chicken warm. The breads underneath the chicken absorb extra juices and are very tasty. Rip off portions of the bread and eat them with the kabobs.

2½ pounds skinless, boneless chicken breasts

1 medium sweet onion, like Vidalia

1½ cups plain yogurt

1 teaspoon salt

¼ teaspoon black pepper

½ tablespoon fresh lemon juice

6 plum tomatoes

1 package pita breads

Up to 48 hours ahead: Trim all visible fat from chicken breasts. Cut chicken breasts into 1-inch cubes. Place chicken in a large nonmetal container. Grate onions in a food processor. Add grated onions and their juices to the chicken cubes. Mix well. Add yogurt, salt, and pepper and mix well. Add lemon juice. Mix well, making sure every piece is covered with the yogurt marinade.

Cover container and marinate at least overnight. (After 24 hours of marinating, chicken-yogurt mixture can be frozen for future use.)

To cook: Preheat grill. Thread chicken on metal skewers so that cubes will lie flat on the grill. Thread plum tomatoes on separate skewers. Grill chicken kabobs 10 minutes, turning twice, until chicken is just cooked through and still juicy. (Do not overcook. Chicken will continue cooking after it is removed from the grill.) Place tomato skewers on grill for the final minute the chicken is cooking.

To serve: Place one layer of pita breads on a serving tray. Remove cooked chicken from skewers and place over the bread. Remove tomatoes from skewers and place around perimeter of the serving platter. Top kabobs with a blanket of pita bread.

(SERVES 6)

Grilled Sirloin Kabobs

The longer these colorful kabobs marinate, the better they are. You can start marinating the steak up to 48 hours ahead.

3 pounds sirloin steak, cut 1½ inches thick

1 (24-ounce) bottle Zesty Italian salad dressing

1 yellow bell pepper

1 red bell pepper

1 large sweet onion, like Vidalia

Up to 48 hours ahead: Cut sirloin steak into 2-inch chunks. Place meat in a freezer-weight zipper bag. Pour all but 1 cup salad dressing into bag. Zipper bag securely and shake bag to coat all sides of meat with dressing. Place bag inside another zipper bag, close bag, and refrigerate until needed.

Cut yellow and red bell peppers into 1½-inch pieces. Cut peeled onion into quarters and separate the layers. Place in a zipper bag and refrigerate. About 12 hours before cooking, pour remaining 1 cup salad dressing over vegetables, reseal bag, and refrigerate until needed.

To cook: Preheat grill. Thread steak, peppers, and onions alternately onto long metal skewers. Place skewers on rack of hot grill. Baste with dressing marinade. Grill skewers for 7 minutes, turning skewers 3 or 4 times. Steak will be medium-rare.

To serve: Serve the kabobs on the skewers or remove meat and vegetables and present them in a tumble on a large serving platter.

Chef's note: For both chicken and sirloin kabobs, use metal skewers whose shafts are flat, not round. That way, the meat pieces stay securely on the skewers and don't rotate around. If using wooden skewers, soak them in water for 30 minutes before threading. This will keep them from burning on the grill.

(SERVES 6)

Plum-Ginger Chicken Wings

Plum sauce is a sweet and tart Chinese condiment made from dried plums, sugar, vinegar, and ginger.

⅔ cup bottled plum sauce

¼ cup thinly sliced scallions

3 tablespoons soy sauce

2 tablespoons rice vinegar

1 tablespoon gingerroot paste or finely grated gingerroot

1 tablespoon honey

¼ teaspoon crushed red pepper flakes

2½ pounds chicken wings

Olive oil spray

Your favorite poultry seasoning blend

Sesame seeds

Up to 3 days ahead: Whisk together plum sauce, scallions, soy sauce, vinegar, gingerroot, honey, and red pepper flakes in a medium bowl. Cover and refrigerate until needed.

Preheat oven to 400 degrees F. Rinse chicken wings and pat them dry. Cut off tips. Coat both sides of wings with olive oil spray. Season generously with your favorite seasoning blend. Coat the bottom of a disposable baking pan with olive oil spray. Place wings, flesh-side down, in pan. Place pan in oven and bake wings for 30 minutes.

Remove pan from oven. Siphon off accumulated grease with a turkey baster. Turn wings over and return pan to oven. Bake wings for 25 minutes more. Remove pan from oven. Spread plum-ginger sauce atop wings. Return pan of wings to oven for 5 more minutes.

Transfer wings to a serving platter. Drizzle wings with plum-ginger sauce. Sprinkle them with sesame seeds. Serve with more plum-ginger sauce on the side.

Chef's note: I use Kikkoman brand plum sauce for this recipe. Two-thirds cup is exactly one (9.3-ounce) jar.

(SERVES 2)

Grill-Roasted Turkey with Orange-Molasses Glaze

Turkey is not just a holiday meal anymore! Once you grill-roast a turkey, you'll never roast one in your oven again. The turkey cooks in half the time recommended for oven roasting and needs your attention only for the final 15 minutes.

1 whole (14- to 16-pound) turkey

Olive oil spray or ¼ cup olive or canola oil

Poultry seasoning rub

1 cup orange juice

1 tablespoon molasses

1 tablespoon white wine vinegar

1 tablespoon dry mustard

Preheat gas grill for 15 minutes with all burners on low heat (400 degrees F). Remove giblets and neck from turkey and discard. Rinse turkey and pat dry. Coat skin of turkey with olive oil spray or brush with oil. Sprinkle your favorite poultry seasoning over entire surface of turkey and rub into skin.

Place turkey in an aluminum foil disposable roasting pan that has been coated with olive oil spray. Place a tent of aluminum foil over turkey and seal tightly. Place pan on the grill rack and close lid. Cook for 3 hours, or until popper is exposed or turkey leg can be pulled away from the body.

Meanwhile, make orange-molasses glaze. Whisk orange juice, molasses, vinegar, and dry mustard together in a small saucepan over medium heat. Bring to a boil and cook for 2 minutes, until glaze reduces slightly. Remove from heat and transfer to a small bowl.

Remove tenting from turkey. Baste turkey with glaze. Close grill lid and cook 15 minutes more, basting every 5 minutes, until bird is golden brown. Remove turkey from grill and allow it to sit 5 minutes. Carve turkey, place on a large platter, and serve immediately.

Chef's note: Do not use a self-basting turkey. Do not open the grill lid to check on the turkey while it is roasting, because you'll cause the heat in the grill to drop significantly, and it will take longer for the bird to cook. You can substitute pomegranate or cranberry juice for the orange juice if desired. Also, you can place your favorite stuffing in the turkey cavity just before grilling. Remove cooked stuffing before carving the turkey.

(SERVES 8 TO 10)

Roast Duck with Fruited Orange Sauce

Ducks are fatty birds. Baking them usually means a lot of splattering grease in the bottom of the pan, which makes many cooks think the process is just too much trouble. Roasting a duck is actually very easy and not messy at all when you stuff the cavities with oranges. The juice from the oranges drips into the pan and keeps the grease from burning.

1 cup orange juice

1 cup orange marmalade

1 tablespoon cornstarch

2 tablespoons fresh lemon juice

2 cups frozen peach slices, cut in ¼-inch dice

2 bananas, sliced in half lengthwise and cut into ¼-inch pieces

1 tablespoon orange liqueur

1 tablespoon grated orange peel

2 whole defrosted frozen ducks, giblets removed

2 large navel oranges

McCormick Garlic and Herb seasoning

Early in the day: Place orange juice and marmalade in a medium nonstick saucepan over medium heat. Stir until marmalade has dissolved, about 1 minute. Whisk cornstarch and lemon juice together in a small bowl. Add to orange juice mixture. Whisk until thickened slightly, about 2 minutes. Stir in peaches, bananas, orange liqueur, and orange peel. Remove from heat. Transfer to a covered container and refrigerate until needed. (Makes 4 cups.)

About 3 hours ahead: Preheat oven to 425 degrees F. Rinse ducks and inner cavities and dry with paper toweling. Cut away excess fat with kitchen scissors, including neck flaps and tails. Cut each orange into eight pieces. Stuff each duck cavity with oranges. Sprinkle all surfaces of each duck liberally with garlic and herb seasoning. Rub seasoning into skin. Transfer ducks to a wire rack placed in a large aluminum roasting pan.

Bake ducks for 30 minutes. Reduce heat to 350 degrees F. Bake for 1½ hours more. Increase heat to 425 degrees F and bake for another 20 minutes, until skin is crispy and juices near leg joint run clear when tested with a knife.

About 15 minutes before serving, place orange sauce in a medium nonstick saucepan over low heat until heated through.

Remove oranges from duck cavities and discard. Cut each duck in half through the breastbone and on either side of the backbone. Discard the backbones. Cut each piece in half again, creating 4 breast/wing quarters and 4 leg/thigh quarters. Serve duck with fruited orange sauce.

Chef's note: You'll need an extra orange for the grated orange peel if you don't already have some on hand in your freezer pantry. After grating the peel, squeeze the orange and use the juice in the sauce.

(SERVES 8)

Live from Up North, It's Friday Night . . . Fish Fry

Nothing says Wisconsin like beer, brats, and cheese—unless it is the Friday Night Fish Fry! The culinary tradition is ubiquitous in the state, with nearly every dining establishment offering some variation of the gustatory event.

What began with the Roman Catholic immigrants' papal-mandated meatless Fridays as a day of abstinence morphed into a bona fide social event by the years of Prohibition in the 1920s. Taverns who were obeying the law, in order to stay afloat financially, marketed the piscatorial meal as a social event to attract families and groups of friends. Fish was plentiful, and it was a cheap, easy way to feed a crowd. (Speakeasies followed suit, offering the fish meal "free," if one purchased their illegal booze.)

By the middle of the twentieth century, even though the Vatican Council had ended the Friday meat ban, the Friday Night Fish Fry was cemented as an undying ritual of Wisconsin's food culture. No hard and fast rules apply to what's served, but culinary traditions generally prevail. Up until the 1960s and 1970s, most of the fish were caught in Lake Michigan or Lake Superior—lake perch, smelts, bluegills, and walleye. But overfishing depleted these species, so cod and haddock became the prevalent alternatives, generally beer-battered and deep-fried. These days, if you encounter offerings of walleye or perch, they generally come from the Canadian waters of Lake Erie. Some restaurants also offer locally caught fish, which are usually lightly breaded and pan-fried.

And for the sides? Always tartar sauce and a wedge of lemon. Always coleslaw and sometimes a side of rye bread. (Back in the day before good deboning practices, a piece of rye bread was served to hold the bones.) Always French fries and sometimes potato pancakes. Often it is "all you can eat," and usually, a fair amount of beer is involved!

Fish and Chips

Lightened from the traditional Friday night fish fry deep-fried standards, these pan-fried tilapia fillets and baked chili and cheese fries are enhanced by a quick, homemade tartar sauce. You can make the sauce and fry the fish while the fries are baking, all in less than 30 minutes.

1 teaspoon chili powder

½ teaspoon coarse salt, divided, plus more

¼ teaspoon dried oregano

½ teaspoon garlic powder, divided

⅛ teaspoon ground cumin

1 tablespoon Parmesan cheese

¼ teaspoon ground black pepper, plus more

1 (32-ounce) package frozen crinkle-cut French-fried potatoes

Olive oil spray

½ cup mayonnaise

2 tablespoons finely chopped sweet pickle

½ tablespoon finely chopped scallions

½ tablespoon finely chopped pimento-stuffed olives

1 teaspoon rice vinegar

1 teaspoon lemon juice

1 large egg

2 teaspoons honey

1 cup seasoned fish breading mix, such as Shore Lunch

¼ cup olive oil

1 pound (4) tilapia fillets, or any firm, white fish fillets

For the fries: Mix chili powder, ¼ teaspoon salt, oregano, ¼ teaspoon garlic powder, and cumin in a small bowl. In another small bowl, mix Parmesan cheese, ¼ teaspoon salt, remaining ¼ teaspoon garlic powder, and ¼ teaspoon black pepper.

Preheat oven to 450 degrees F. Line a baking sheet with aluminum foil. Coat foil with olive oil spray. Place fries on foil and coat all sides with olive oil spray. Sprinkle chili seasoning atop half the fries, cheese seasoning atop the other half. Toss to coat fries well with seasonings. Bake for 10 minutes. Turn fries and bake 10 minutes more.

For the tartar sauce: While fries are baking, mix mayonnaise, sweet pickle, scallions, olives, vinegar, lemon juice, and pinch of coarse salt together in a small bowl. Refrigerate until needed. (Makes ⅔ cup.)

For the fish: Whisk egg and honey together in a shallow bowl. Place breading mix on a dinner plate. Place 2 tablespoons oil in each of 2 large nonstick skillets over medium heat. Dip both sides of each fish fillet in egg mixture and then coat both sides with breading. Place in skillet and cook for 2 minutes. Turn fillets with a firm spatula. Cook for 1 to 2 minutes longer, until fish is golden and flakes with a fork.

Serve fried fish with tartar sauce, chili fries, and cheese fries.

Chef's note: Shore Lunch suggests marinating fish fillets in yellow mustard, hot sauce, and granulated garlic before tossing them with the breading if you want to spice things up a bit.

(SERVES 4)

Grilled Bruschetta Walleye Fillets

The dueling flavors in the grilled bruschetta add a spark to every bite of this grilled walleye.

⅔ cup chopped onions

¼ cup plus 2 tablespoons capers, rinsed and drained

½ cup minced shallots

2 cups quartered grape tomatoes

2 tablespoons plus 2 teaspoons snipped fresh basil

¼ cup fresh lemon juice

¼ cup plus 2 tablespoons olive oil

1 teaspoon salt

½ teaspoon cracked black pepper

2 to 2½-pounds walleye fillets or other firm white fish fillets, such as grouper or tilapia

Olive oil spray

At least 1 hour or up to 4 hours ahead: In a medium covered container, combine onions, capers, shallots, tomatoes, basil, lemon juice, olive oil, salt, and pepper. Stir to mix well. Refrigerate to allow flavors to marry.

Preheat grill to 400 degrees F. Cut each walleye fillet into 2 pieces. Coat fish with olive oil spray. Coat a Teflon fish grill rack with vegetable cooking spray. Place walleye on rack, skin-side down. Top with half the tomato mixture. Cook for 7 minutes. Add remaining bruschetta topping. Cook 8 minutes, or until fish is just cooked through and flakes with a fork. Serve immediately.

Chef's note: Frozen Canadian walleye fillets are increasing available in fish markets and supermarkets, especially in Wisconsin. The fillets are very large. If you substitute other smaller white fish fillets, do not cut the fillets into 2 pieces.

(SERVES 4)

GETTY IMAGES

Grilled Marinated Swordfish

The marinade gives this swordfish the grilled cross-hatch marks you'd find in a fine sea-food restaurant. If your grill doesn't have a thermostat, just use the hottest setting.

2 tablespoons soy sauce

¼ cup orange juice

2 tablespoons ketchup

2 tablespoons snipped fresh flat leaf parsley

1 tablespoon fresh lemon juice

½ teaspoon black pepper

1 teaspoon garlic paste or finely minced garlic

2 pounds fresh swordfish, cut 1½ inches thick

Two hours ahead: Mix soy sauce, orange juice, ketchup, parsley, lemon juice, pepper, and garlic together in a medium bowl. Rinse swordfish and dry with paper toweling. Pour half the marinade in a shallow dish. Place swordfish atop marinade. Pour remaining marinade over swordfish. Cover and refrigerate until needed.

Preheat gas grill to 550 degrees F (hot grill). Remove swordfish from marinade. Place marinade in a microwave-safe container and heat for 1 minute. Place swordfish on grill. Brush with marinade. Grill swordfish for 5½ minutes. Turn swordfish and brush with marinade. Grill for 5½ minutes more. (Fish should have just lost its translucency; do not overcook or fish will be dry.) Brush with marinade before serving. Serve immediately.

Chef's note: You can use this marinade on other fish as well. But if using a flaky white fish, marinade the fish for no more than 30 minutes. Adjust grilling time according to the thickness of the fish.

(SERVES 4)

Lake Trout Piccata

Lake trout aren't actually considered trout, but char, a member of the salmon family. Arctic char is its closest relative. They are plentiful in Lake Superior, upon which Northern Wisconsin borders. More than 80 species of fish are found in Lake Superior, which is the largest freshwater lake in the world (by surface area).

Almond flour

Salt and freshly ground black pepper

1 tablespoon light olive oil

1 tablespoon butter

1 pound (¾-inch thick) lake trout fillets or other fish fillets

2 tablespoons capers

¼ cup dry white wine

¼ cup lemon juice

1 lemon, very thinly sliced

Place flour on a large plate and season with salt and pepper.

Heat a heavy skillet, big enough to hold the fish fillets, over medium heat. When hot, add olive oil and butter. Dredge fish in seasoned flour on both sides. When butter has melted completely, add the fish to the pan skin-side up. Cook for 3 to 5 minutes, depending upon the thickness of the fish, or until golden brown on the bottom. Use two spatulas to carefully flip the fish, so that the skin side is down.

Mix together capers, white wine, and lemon juice and add to the pan next to the fish along with the lemon slices. Cook another few minutes or until the wine has reduced, the lemon slices are beginning to caramelize, and the fish is cooked through. Serve fish immediately, with the sauce, lemons, and capers on top.

(SERVES 2)

Salmon in Puff Pastry

Call it salmon en croute, and your party guests will think they are eating in a French restaurant. This special occasion dish requires a mere 30-minute prep time but looks and tastes like a chef-prepared creation.

1 (17.3-ounce) package puff pastry (2 sheets)

1 (2½- to 3-pound) skinless salmon fillet

½ teaspoon salt

½ teaspoon black pepper

2 (5.2-ounce) packages Boursin garlic and herb cheese spread

1 (9-ounce) package fresh baby spinach, chopped (about 4 packed cups)

1 large egg, beaten with 2 tablespoons water

Early in the day: Place one sheet of puff pastry on a floured surface. Using a rolling pin, roll pastry to form a 10- x 18-inch rectangle. Transfer rolled pastry to a baking sheet. Place salmon atop pastry. (Make sure you have about ¾-inch pastry surrounding salmon on all sides.) Sprinkle salmon with salt and pepper.

Spread cheese over the top and sides of the salmon. Top with chopped spinach, pressing spinach into the cheese and mounding the excess on top. Brush egg wash on pastry surrounding salmon.

Roll remaining sheet of pastry to the same size as the first. Place atop the salmon. Cut excess from bottom layer of pastry and reserve. Press pastry edges together and roll to form a sealed border around salmon. Brush pastry with egg wash. (Roll out pastry scraps, if desired, and cut them into decorative shapes with small cookie cutters. Place them on top of the encased salmon and brush with egg wash.) Cover pastry-encased salmon with cling wrap and aluminum foil and refrigerate until needed.

To bake: Preheat oven to 400 degrees F. Bring salmon to room temperature (about 30 minutes before baking.) Bake for 30 minutes, until pastry is golden. Transfer salmon to a large serving platter. Cut into 1½-inch-wide slices, then cut each slice in half.

Chef's note: You can allow this dish to cool after baking and then refrigerate it until needed. Serve it at room temperature. For a small group, use individual salmon fillets and follow the procedure above, using puff pastry sheets cut to size.

(SERVES 16 TO 20)

Stir Fry Your Way

A good stir fry is made up of five components: meat/seafood, marinade/sauce, aromatics, vegetables, and garnish. Mix and match ingredients from the choices below to design your own stir-fry creation. Follow the stir-fry technique described in the recipe that follows and serve stir fry over steamed short- or medium-grain rice, Chinese egg noodles, or Thai rice noodles. Figure that is about 3 ounces meat/4 ounces seafood, 1 cup vegetables, and 1 cup cooked rice per person (1 cup uncooked rice equals 3 cups cooked). The keys to a great stir fry are to have all your ingredients prepped and ready before you start and to cook over high heat, stirring constantly.

SHUTTERSTOCK

Stir Fry for Four

MEAT/SEAFOOD:

Cut 12 ounces flank steak, pork tenderloin, or boneless chicken breasts into ¼-inch slices across grain, then into ½-inch strips lengthwise. When using seafood, increase amount to 1 pound and leave shrimp or scallops whole. Cook meat or chicken in batches so as not to crowd the pieces in the wok.

MARINADE/SAUCE:

The marinade/sauce is made up of liquid, flavorings, sweetener, and cornstarch. Whisk together a total of ½ cup liquid (sherry, citrus juice, rice or white wine, broth) with a total of 2 tablespoons flavorings (chili sauce with garlic, sweet Asian chili sauce, soy sauce, hoisin sauce, oyster sauce, citrus peel, peanut butter, fish sauce, toasted sesame oil), 1 tablespoon sweetener (honey, white sugar, brown sugar), and 1 tablespoon cornstarch.

AROMATICS:

1 tablespoon garlic paste or finely minced garlic and 1 tablespoon gingerroot paste or finely minced gingerroot.

VEGETABLES:

Use 4 cups of bite-size vegetables—frozen or fresh. Frozen Asian vegetable medley is usually already cut into bite-size pieces and cooks uniformly in about 3 minutes. Fresh vegetables fall into three categories of cooking times: slow, medium, and fast. Add slow-cooking vegetables first, cooking for about 3 to 4 minutes. Then add medium-cooking vegetables and cook about 2 to 3 minutes. Add fast-cooking vegetables at the very end of the stir fry and cook for only about 30 seconds.

Slow-cooking vegetables include asparagus, broccoli, carrots, green beans, onions, and winter squash. Medium cooking vegetables include bell peppers, celery, mushrooms, zucchini, and summer squash. Fast cooking vegetables include bean sprouts, cabbage, pea pods, scallions, spinach, and tomatoes.

GARNISHES:

Add garnishes to taste: fresh chopped parsley, chopped toasted nuts, toasted sesame seeds.

Orange Shrimp Stir Fry over Jasmine Rice

Slightly spicy, slightly sweet, and faintly orangey, this stir-fry touches all your taste buds. For a more economical dish, substitute 12 ounces boneless chicken breast for the shrimp.

1½ cups water

1 cup uncooked jasmine rice

1 pound (16–20 count) shrimp

2 tablespoons sesame seeds

¼ cup orange juice

2 tablespoons sherry

2 tablespoons rice vinegar

1 tablespoon orange marmalade

1 tablespoon sweet Asian chili sauce

1 tablespoon honey

1 tablespoon cornstarch

¼ cup canola oil, divided

1 tablespoon garlic paste or minced garlic

1 tablespoon gingerroot paste or minced gingerroot

4 cups frozen Asian mixed vegetables, cut into uniform bite-size pieces

Place water in a medium saucepan over high heat. When water comes to a boil, stir in rice. Reduce heat to low, place 2 pieces of paper toweling over pan, place cover on saucepan, and simmer for 15 minutes, until water is absorbed. Fluff rice with a fork before serving.

While rice is cooking, peel and devein shrimp. Place sesame seeds in a small nonstick skillet over low heat. Toast them, stirring frequently, for about 1 minute. Remove from heat and set aside.

Whisk together orange juice, sherry, vinegar, marmalade, chili sauce, honey, and cornstarch in a medium bowl. Add shrimp and stir until shrimp are coated with sauce.

Heat 2 tablespoons oil in a large wok or stir fry pan over high heat. Transfer shrimp from sauce to a plate with a slotted spoon. Add shrimp to hot oil, stirring constantly, until shrimp is pink and nearly cooked through, 1½ to 2 minutes. Remove shrimp to a plate and set aside until needed.

Add 1 tablespoon oil to wok. Add garlic and gingerroot and cook, stirring constantly, for 15 seconds. Add remaining 1 tablespoon oil and frozen vegetables to wok and stir fry, stirring constantly for 2 minutes. Stir in orange sauce and cook for 1 minute more, until sauce begins to thicken. Add shrimp and toss with vegetables. Cook for 1 minute, stirring constantly, until shrimp is heated through and coated with sauce.

Serve immediately over jasmine rice. Sprinkle each serving with toasted sesame seeds.

(SERVES 4)

Barbecued Jumbo Shrimp

Jumbo shrimp are called "10–15s" because there are usually ten to fifteen shrimp to a pound. Meatier than most shrimp, they are the perfect size for grilling.

¼ cup chopped sweet onions, like Vidalia

½ cup ketchup

1 tablespoon brown sugar

1 tablespoon dry mustard

¼ teaspoon garlic powder

1 tablespoon white vinegar

2¼ pounds jumbo shrimp (10–15s), peeled and deveined

1 lemon, cut into 8 wedges

One hour ahead: Coat a small nonstick skillet with vegetable cooking spray. Place over medium heat. Add onions and sauté for 1 minute, stirring constantly. Remove skillet from heat. Stir in ketchup, brown sugar, dry mustard, garlic powder, and vinegar.

Rinse shrimp and pat them dry with paper toweling. Place shrimp in a covered container. Pour barbecue sauce over shrimp and toss shrimp until all are well coated with sauce. Cover and refrigerate for 1 hour.

Preheat gas grill to medium (about 400 degrees). Coat 4 large metal skewers with vegetable cooking spray. Thread shrimp onto skewers, tail to top. Place barbecue sauce in a microwave-safe container. Heat in microwave for 1 minute on high. Grill shrimp skewers for 5 minutes. Turn skewers over and baste with barbecue sauce. Grill another 5 minutes, just until shrimp have lost their translucency when tested with a knife. Remove shrimp from skewers and place in a serving platter. Garnish with lemon wedges. Serve immediately.

Chef's note: You'll have 30 to 32 shrimp with the poundage indicated above, which is about 5 shrimp per person.

(SERVES 6)

SHUTTERSTOCK

Lemon-Sauced Crab Cakes

Blue crabs are so named because of their blue-tinted claws. They are bottom dwellers, eating small fish, snails, mussels, even other blue crabs. They live from one to four years in the wild. The average blue crab only yields about two ounces of crabmeat, so it takes a lot of blue crabs to make a pound!

¾ cup dry white wine

¾ cup chicken broth

¼ cup fresh lemon juice

2 teaspoons cornstarch

1½ teaspoons sugar

4 tablespoons (½ stick) butter, divided

1 pound Phillips pasteurized blue crabmeat (backfin or lump grade), rinsed and patted dry

⅓ cup mayonnaise

½ cup thinly sliced scallions

¼ cup minced red bell peppers

¼ cup thinly sliced celery

2 tablespoons Dijon mustard

1 clove garlic, minced

⅛ teaspoon cayenne pepper

2 large eggs, beaten

¼ cup fresh breadcrumbs

1 lemon, quartered, for garnish

To make lemon sauce: Place wine and broth in a 2-quart saucepan over medium-high heat. Bring to a boil and cook about 8 minutes, stirring frequently, until mixture reduces by half (about ¾ cup). Mix together lemon juice, cornstarch, and sugar in a small bowl and slowly stir it into broth mixture. Keep stirring until sauce boils again. Stir in 2 tablespoons butter. Reduce heat to low, cover saucepan, and keep sauce warm.

To make crab cakes: Place crabmeat, mayonnaise, scallions, bell peppers, celery, mustard, garlic, and cayenne pepper in a large bowl. Stir to mix well. Mix beaten eggs thoroughly into crab mixture. Add breadcrumbs and stir to mix well.

To cook crab cakes: Melt 1 tablespoon butter in each of two 10-inch nonstick skillets over medium heat. Place 6 mounds of crab mixture in each skillet using the serving spoon from your cutlery set as a measure. Flatten each mound into a cake with the back of the spoon. Cook 4 minutes. Carefully turn each cake over. (The cakes tenuously hold together because only a scant amount of breadcrumbs are used in this recipe.) Cook an additional 2 minutes or until the underside is nicely browned.

To serve: Place 3 crab cakes on each dinner plate. Spoon lemon sauce around crab cakes. Garnish with lemon wedges.

(SERVES 4)

Mabel Lake is an 18-acre lake in Vilas County. GETTY IMAGES

Farmers' Market

Salad Bowl

A wedge of iceberg lettuce topped with bottled blue cheese dressing may still be comfort food to many, but the twenty-first-century salad bowl offers many more options. The wide availability of mixed baby greens and fresh herbs, specialty oils and vinegars, year-round veggies and fruits, flavored cheeses, and a global array of seeds and nuts creates a limitless palette from which to paint a salad masterpiece.

You're the artist. Possibilities are endless. Combine your favorite blend of greens and chopped vegetables, add a little cheese, some toasted nuts or seeds, and maybe a sprinkling of fresh or dried fruits. Then toss it all together with a homemade salad dressing.

Making your own fresh salad dressing is quick, easy, fun, and economical. The taste is superior to that of bottled dressings and more nutritious as well. Forget preservatives and chemical ingredients you can't identify. It will take you less than 10 minutes to mix up any one of the dressings below, which each makes enough to dress several large salads and will keep in the refrigerator for one to two weeks.

Honey-Mustard Vinaigrette

You can substitute more exotic vinegars, such as chardonnay or champagne vinegar in this recipe, if you have them on hand and your budget allows.

1 tablespoon Dijon mustard

2 tablespoons rice wine vinegar

2 tablespoons honey

¼ teaspoon salt

⅛ teaspoon ground white pepper

¼ cup extra-virgin olive oil

Place mustard, vinegar, honey, salt, and pepper in a small bowl. Beat with a wire whisk until well blended. Slowly add the olive oil, whisking constantly. Transfer to a covered container and refrigerate until needed.

(MAKES ABOUT ½ CUP)

Raspberry Vinaigrette

When raspberries are in season and reasonably priced, freeze them on parchment-paper-lined baking sheets until solid, then pop them into labeled zipper bags and store them in the freezer until needed.

¼ cup fresh or frozen raspberries

2 tablespoons chopped onions

2 tablespoons rice wine vinegar

¼ teaspoon celery seed

1½ teaspoons dry mustard

¼ teaspoon salt

2 tablespoons plus 2 teaspoons honey

¼ cup extra-virgin olive oil

Place raspberries, onions, vinegar, celery seed, dry mustard, salt, and honey in a blender. Pulse until well mixed and raspberries are pureed. With blender on low, slowly add olive oil. Transfer dressing to a covered container and refrigerate until needed, up to 1 week.

(MAKES ABOUT ¾ CUP)

Lemon-Poppy Seed Dressing

This light dressing is fantastic tossed with a salad of romaine lettuce, shredded Swiss cheese, cashews, dried cranberries, and diced apples and pears.

¼ cup sugar

¼ cup fresh lemon juice

1 teaspoon finely minced sweet onions, like Vidalia

½ teaspoon Dijon mustard

¼ teaspoon salt

⅓ cup olive oil

½ tablespoon poppy seeds

Place sugar, lemon juice, onions, mustard, and salt in a small mixing bowl. Whisk until sugar has dissolved. Slowly pour in olive oil, whisking constantly until mixture is smooth. Whisk in poppy seeds. Transfer to a covered container and refrigerate until needed, up to 1 week. Bring to room temperature before serving.

(MAKES ABOUT ¾ CUP)

Blue Cheese Dressing

Okay, okay. It may be a bit pricier than the other salad dressings, but don't we all occasionally still yearn for a comforting wedge of iceberg lettuce topped with a thick glob of blue cheese dressing? Homemade is the best!

¼ cup mayonnaise

3 tablespoons sour cream

2 teaspoons milk

½ teaspoon Worcestershire sauce

1 tablespoon rice vinegar

1 teaspoon lemon juice

¼ teaspoon dry mustard

¼ teaspoon salt

¼ teaspoon black pepper

½ teaspoon sugar

½ cup crumbled blue cheese

Whisk mayonnaise, sour cream, and milk together in a medium bowl. Whisk in Worcestershire sauce, vinegar, lemon juice, dry mustard, salt, black pepper, and sugar. Add blue cheese and stir until creamy and well mixed. Transfer to a covered container and refrigerate until needed, up to 1 week. (If dressing gets too thick, thin it by whisking in a little milk.)

(MAKES ABOUT 3/4 CUP)

Endive and Pear Salad with Champagne Vinaigrette

Belgian Endive is a small, delicately flavored, slightly bitter cylindrical head of lettuce with pale yellow leaves. It is grown just beneath the soil in dark rooms, much like mushrooms, to keep it pale.

1 large Belgian endive, leaves washed and spun dry

1 firm, ripe pear, halved, cored, and cut into ¼-inch-thick slices

2 tablespoons crumbled Roquefort or blue cheese

2 teaspoons mayonnaise

1 teaspoon Dijon mustard

2 teaspoons champagne or white wine vinegar

1 teaspoon water

Salt and freshly ground black pepper

2 tablespoons extra-virgin olive oil

¼ cup pine nuts, dry toasted

Cut endive leaves lengthwise into thin strips, then cut strips in half crosswise. Cut pear slices in half crosswise.

Divide the endive between 2 salad plates. Arrange the pear slices atop the endive. Sprinkle salads with Roquefort cheese.

In a small bowl, whisk together mayonnaise, mustard, vinegar, water, and salt and pepper to taste. Add olive oil in a stream, whisking until it is emulsified. Drizzle dressing over salads. Sprinkle salads with pine nuts.

(SERVES 2)

Hot Apple Slaw

About 60 million pounds of more than three hundred varieties apples are grown in Wisconsin a year. Bayfield, way, way Up North on the shores of Lake Superior, holds a notable three-day festival every October, celebrating all things apple. (See Way Up North Fruit Loop sidebar, page 184.)

½ cup brown sugar

⅓ cup apple cider vinegar

1½ tablespoons canola oil

¼ teaspoon salt

¼ teaspoon black pepper

2 cups diced Honeycrisp or other tart-sweet apples

1 (12-ounce) package broccoli slaw

⅔ cup dried tart cherries

3 tablespoons roasted, salted sunflower seeds

Mix brown sugar, vinegar, oil, salt, and pepper together in a small bowl. Place apples, broccoli slaw, cherries, and sunflower seeds in a large skillet over medium heat. Pour vinaigrette over broccoli mixture. Cook, stirring frequently, until vinaigrette has evaporated but vegetables are still slightly crunchy. Serve immediately.

(SERVES 8)

Rainbow Summer Tomato Salad

Summer is the time for a panoply of wonderful tomatoes of all colors. This salad is beyond simple and allows the tomatoes' unique flavors to shine through.

1 red tomato

1 orange tomato

1 yellow tomato

1 green tomato, turning slight ripe so it looks a little streaky

Salt and freshly ground black pepper

1 to 1½ tablespoons really good balsamic vinegar, like Villa Manodori

1 tablespoon extra-virgin olive oil

Core each tomato and cut into 8 wedges. Place wedges in a serving bowl and salt and pepper them generously. Drizzle balsamic vinegar and olive oil over tomatoes and toss to combine. Season again with salt and pepper to taste.

Chef's note: I always keep a bottle of Villa Manodori brand Aceto Balsamico de Modina in my pantry. It is pricy—$35 to $40 a bottle—so I only use it as a special drizzle atop foods, such as tomatoes. Its dark, rich color, syrupy consistency, and sweet vinegary flavor is unique among balsamics.

(SERVES 4 TO 6)

The Three Sisters

The three sisters—corn, climbing beans, and winter squash—enjoy a symbiotic relationship.
SHUTTERSTOCK

The three sisters—corn, climbing beans, and winter squash—form a triad that was an essential part of the foodways and culture of the early Ojibwe (Chippewa) tribes of northern Wisconsin and other indigenous peoples in the state. Always planted together in the same mound, the three vegetables enjoyed a symbiotic relationship. The beans, which provide nitrogen to the soil, were planted at the base of the corn, the stalks of which provided a trellis-type support for the climbing bean vines. The large leaves of the squash, planted surrounding the corn and beans, shaded the ground, a kind of living mulch, helping to retain moisture and prevent weeds.

The three sisters are traditionally planted from seed. Sister Corn is planted first. Sister Bean is planted when Sister Corn is a few inches high, a couple of weeks later. Finally, Sister Squash is planted about a week after Sister Bean sprouts up. Growing together, they enrich the soil and deter pests.

The three sisters complement each other when combined for the culinary table as well. Corn provides carbohydrates, beans the protein, and squash offers other vitamins and minerals not found in the corn and beans.

VICTORIA SHEARER

Three Sisters Salad

¼ cup plus 1 tablespoon light olive oil, divided

¾ cup fresh butternut squash, cut in ½-inch dice

Salt and freshly ground black pepper

2½ cups cooked fresh or frozen corn

1 (14.5-ounce) can black beans, rinsed and drained

½ cup chopped sweet onions

½ cup chopped red bell peppers

2 tablespoons fresh snipped dill

1 teaspoon garlic paste or 1 clove garlic, minced

3 tablespoons apple cider vinegar

At least 2 hours ahead: Heat 1 tablespoon oil in a large sauté pan over medium-high heat. Add squash and sauté, stirring frequently, until just cooked through. (Test squash pieces with a fork; it should easily pierce. Do not overcook.) Transfer squash to a large plate and allow it to cool. Season with salt and pepper to taste.

Place corn, black beans, onions, and bell peppers in a large bowl. Season with salt and pepper to taste. Add cooled squash and snipped dill. Toss ingredients. Adjust seasonings.

In a small bowl, whisk garlic paste into vinegar. Slowly add remaining ¼ cup olive oil, whisking constantly. Pour dressing over vegetables and toss to combine. Cover and refrigerate at least 1 hour before serving.

Chef's note: Buy butternut squash already cut into chunks at your supermarket. Cut into small dice for this recipe.

(SERVES A CROWD)

Spinach Salad with Warm Bacon Dressing

5 slices bacon

⅓ cup red wine vinegar

3 tablespoons orange juice

¼ cup honey

¼ teaspoon salt

⅛ teaspoon black pepper

1 (9-ounce) bag baby spinach, washed and spun dry

½ cup thinly sliced button mushrooms

¼ cup thinly sliced red onions

Cook bacon in a large nonstick skillet over medium heat until crispy. Remove bacon to drain on paper toweling. Reserve 1 tablespoon bacon grease and discard the rest. Crumble bacon and set aside.

Place reserved bacon grease in skillet over medium-low heat. Add vinegar, orange juice, honey, salt, and pepper. Cook until heated through, stirring occasionally, about 1 minute. Add bacon and cook 1 minute more.

Place spinach, mushrooms, and onions in a large salad bowl. Spoon dressing (to taste) over greens and toss to combine. Divide salad among individual salad plates. Top with remaining bacon crumbles from the dressing.

(SERVES 4 TO 6)

"The Gang's All Here" Salad

This hearty salad feeds a family reunion, which happens often during an Up North summer. Cut the ingredients in half for a smaller family gathering.

1 head cauliflower, divided into florets

1 bunch broccoli, divided into florets

1 large sweet onion, like Vidalia, coarsely chopped

10 slices of bacon, cooked, drained, crumbled

2 cups shredded cheddar cheese

6 hard-boiled eggs, coarsely chopped

¾ cup raisins

1 cup mayonnaise

¼ cup white wine vinegar

½ cup sugar

1 teaspoon salt

½ teaspoon pepper

At least four hours and up to one day ahead: In a large bowl, place cauliflower, broccoli, onions, bacon, cheese, eggs, and raisins. Toss to mix. In a small bowl, stir mayonnaise, vinegar, sugar, salt, and pepper to mix well. Add dressing to salad and toss to mix. Refrigerate for 4 hours or overnight to marry flavors.

(SERVES 12 TO 16)

Versatile Vegetables

A perfectly steamed vegetable tossed or drizzled with a tasty sauce adds a flavorful, healthful boost to any meal. Next, you'll find four versatile vegetables and four yummy topper sauces. Mix and match any way you choose. All sauces can be made ahead and refrigerated until needed. Reheat on low heat or microwave for 30 seconds to 1 minute before serving.

Asparagus

Asparagus deteriorates fairly quickly. Wrap damp paper toweling around its stems and store in a plastic zipper bag in the refrigerator. It will last several days. Clean asparagus under running water, bending the stalks until each naturally snaps. Discard the woody ends. Large asparagus, which is more mature and less tender, may need to be peeled with a vegetable peeler.

To steam: Place asparagus in a medium skillet. Cover with water. Place skillet over medium-high heat and cook about 3 minutes (thin asparagus), or until crisp-tender when tested with a fork. Remove from heat. Drain, rinse with cold water, and drain again.

Place asparagus on a serving platter. Drizzle with choice of sauces below. Serve asparagus hot or at room temperature.

Green Beans

Place cleaned beans in a vegetable steamer over 2 inches of water in a large saucepan. Steam beans over medium-high heat for 5 minutes, or until beans are crisp-tender when tested with a fork. Drain, rinse with cold water, and drain again.

Place green beans on a serving platter. Drizzle with choice of sauces below.

Baby Carrots

Cut baby carrots in quarters, lengthwise. Place carrots with water to cover in a medium saucepan over high heat. When water comes to a boil, reduce heat to medium. Cook for 8 to 10 minutes, until carrots are cooked through but still slightly crunchy. Drain, rinse with cold water, and drain again. Return carrots to saucepan and toss with choice of sauces below. Place dressed carrots on a serving platter.

Sugar Snap Peas

Cut stem ends from sugar snap peas. Place a large saucepan of water over high heat. When water comes to a boil, add peas. Cook for 30 seconds only. Drain, rinse with cold water, and drain again. Place peas in a serving bowl and toss with choice of sauces below.

Sauces

Lemon-Mustard Sauce

3 tablespoons butter

1½ teaspoons fresh lemon juice

1½ teaspoons Dijon mustard

Melt butter in microwave for 1 minute. Whisk in lemon juice and mustard. Drizzle over steamed vegetables.

(MAKES ¼ CUP)

Ginger-Hoisin Sauce

2 tablespoons rice wine vinegar

1 tablespoon gingerroot paste or finely grated fresh gingerroot

2 tablespoons hoisin sauce

¼ cup chopped scallions

Place vinegar, gingerroot, hoisin sauce, and scallions in a small bowl. Whisk to mix. You can prepare the ginger-hoisin sauce up to 3 days ahead. Place in a covered container and refrigerate until needed. Bring sauce to room temperature before drizzling on hot veggies.

(MAKES ⅓ CUP)

Sesame-Orange Sauce

1½ tablespoons sesame seeds

¼ cup frozen orange juice concentrate, thawed

2 tablespoons Dijon mustard

⅓ cup red currant jelly

1½ tablespoons red wine vinegar

Dash cayenne pepper

1½ tablespoons olive oil

Place sesame seeds in a small skillet over medium-low heat until lightly toasted, about 2 minutes. Shake pan occasionally.

Meanwhile, place orange juice concentrate, mustard, jelly, vinegar, and pepper in a small saucepan over medium-low heat. Whisk until jelly has melted and mixture is bubbly. Remove from heat and whisk in oil and sesame seeds. Drizzle over steamed vegetables.

(MAKES ¾ CUP)

Fresh Herb–Butter Sauce

4 tablespoons butter

½ cup minced sweet onions, like Vidalia

½ teaspoon garlic paste or finely minced garlic

¼ cup finely minced celery

½ cup snipped fresh parsley

1 teaspoon snipped fresh rosemary

1 teaspoon snipped fresh basil

¼ teaspoon kosher salt

Melt butter in a medium nonstick skillet over medium heat. Add onions, garlic, and celery and sauté until onions are soft but celery is still slightly crunchy, about 3 minutes. Stir in parsley, rosemary, basil, and salt and cook for 1 minute more. Drizzle over steamed vegetables.

(MAKES ½ CUP)

Baked Goat Cheese Stuffed Tomatoes

France is the world's leading producer of goat cheese. Wisconsin's own Montchevre, made in Preston, Wisconsin, according to French traditions, is now the leading goat cheese brand in the United States.

4 large tomatoes

Salt and freshly ground black pepper

1 tablespoon extra-virgin olive oil, plus more for drizzling

4 ounces honey goat cheese

¼ cup unseasoned Japanese panko breadcrumbs

1 tablespoon grated Parmesan cheese

1 tablespoon chopped fresh parsley

½ teaspoon garlic paste or grated fresh garlic

¼ teaspoon dried thyme

½ teaspoon grated lemon zest

¼ teaspoon kosher salt

Preheat oven to 400 degrees F. Cut off the tops of tomatoes and save for another use. With a small spoon, scoop out all the seeds of the tomatoes. Turn tomatoes over and place on paper toweling to drain. Season interior of tomatoes with salt and pepper. Drizzle with olive oil. Fill each tomato with 1 ounce goat cheese. In a small bowl, combine breadcrumbs, 1 tablespoon olive oil, Parmesan cheese, parsley, garlic, thyme, lemon zest and kosher salt. Sprinkle generously over stuffed tomatoes.

Place tomatoes in a shallow baking dish. Bake tomatoes for 10 minutes, until crumbs are browned. Serve immediately.

(SERVES 4)

Candied Carrots

Petite baby carrots are the tiniest carrots now on the market—no bigger than your pinky finger and very sweet. Some carrots are marketed as "baby-cut" carrots. These are not the same as baby carrots. Baby-cut carrots are large, regular carrots that have been cut and rounded by machine to a small size to look like a baby carrot. If you use baby-cut carrots instead of the smaller version, cut them in half.

4 cups petite baby carrots

⅓ cup butter

⅓ cup jellied cranberry sauce

¼ cup brown sugar

Salt and freshly ground black pepper

1 tablespoon snipped fresh dill

Place carrots in a large saucepan with water to cover. Bring water to a boil and cook over medium heat until carrots are crisp tender, about 3 minutes. (Test carrots frequently with a fork.) Drain carrots in a colander. Rinse with cold water and drain again.

Meanwhile, place butter, cranberry sauce, and brown sugar in a small nonstick saucepan over low heat. Cook, stirring frequently, until all ingredients have melted and are well blended, 2 to 3 minutes.

Place drained carrots back in saucepan over low heat. Pour butter sauce over carrots and toss until they are well coated. Season with salt and freshly ground black pepper to taste. Sprinkle with fresh dill. Serve immediately.

(SERVES 8 TO 10)

GETTY IMAGES

Roasted Butternut Squash and Sweet Potato–Pesto Mash

Beige skinned and vase shaped, butternut squash is an orange-fleshed winter squash with a sweet, nutty flavor similar to that of pumpkin.

3 pounds butternut squash, halved and seeded

2 large sweet potatoes (about 1 pound)

½ cup mayonnaise

1 large egg, beaten

1 tablespoon brown sugar

¼ teaspoon salt

¼ teaspoon black pepper

¼ cup prepared basil pesto

½ cup Japanese panko breadcrumbs

¼ cup grated Parmesan cheese

2 tablespoons melted butter

Up to one day ahead: Preheat oven to 350 degrees F. Line a large baking sheet with aluminum foil. Place squash, cut-side down, on foil. Place sweet potatoes on baking sheet. Bake for 1 hour, until vegetables are baked through and soft. Remove from oven and allow them to cool for 10 minutes.

Meanwhile, mix mayonnaise, egg, brown sugar, salt, and pepper together in a small bowl. Scoop squash and sweet potatoes from skins and place in a large bowl. Mash with a spoon until smooth. Pour off any accumulated liquids. Stir in mayonnaise mixture until smooth.

Coat a 2-quart ovenproof serving bowl or baking dish with vegetable cooking spray. Place half the squash mixture in dish. Using a small spoon, dollop 2 table-spoons pesto over squash mixture. Place remaining squash in bowl. Top with dollops of remaining pesto. Use a metal skewer to swirl the pesto through the squash mixture in a decorative fashion.

Mix breadcrumbs and Parmesan cheese together in a medium bowl. Pour in melted butter and mix with a fork until crumbs are well-coated with butter. Sprinkle buttered crumbs atop squash mixture. Cover with cling wrap and refrigerate until needed.

To bake: Preheat oven to 350 degrees F. Remove cling wrap from baking dish and bake, uncovered, for 35 to 45 minutes, until squash is heated through and top is slightly browned.

Chef's note: Use yellow-fleshed sweet potatoes in this recipe. Be sure to drain off as much liquid as possible from the mashed butternut squash and sweet potatoes.

(SERVES 8 TO 10)

Morel Mushroom Foraging

Northern Wisconsin public forests are prime morel mushroom foraging territory. Chequamegon-Nicolet National Forest covers more than 1.5 million acres of woodlands. The Chequamegon side of the forest covers about 858,400 acres in Ashland, Bayfield, Sawyer, Price, Taylor, and Vilas counties. The Nicolet side of the forest covers almost 661,400 acres in Florence, Forest, Langlade, Oconto, Oneida, and Vilas counties. Brule River State Forest in Douglas County, at 47,000 acres, also is a good hunting ground for the wild food treasures.

The highly sought after, edible morel mushrooms emerge from the forest floor from late March until May. The black morel (*Morchella augusticeps*) appears first in the spring and is slightly darker and smaller than the common morel (*Morchella esculenta*), which appears around May. The morel foraging season lasts only four to five weeks. Night temperature must be around 40 degrees F, while daytime temperatures should be between 60 and 70 degrees F. Ground temperatures should be between 50 and 60 degrees F. Morels grow best in weather that is a balanced mixture of sun and rain. Too much or too little rain will ruin the season.

Morels are typically found growing in sandy soils in leaf litter near ash, aspen, elm, and oak trees. They are also found near dying or dead hickory trees and in old orchards. The morel mushroom is the fruiting body that the fungus uses to spread its spores.

The morel foraging season lasts only four to five weeks. SHUTTERSTOCK

Sometimes nicknamed the molly moocher, miracle, hickory chicken, and dryland fish, a true morel can be gray, yellow, and black in color. It is identified by its deeply ridged conical cap that looks like a honeycomb attached to a thick white stalk. When sliced lengthwise, it is hollow from the top of the cap to the tip of the stem.

It is important to properly identify the morel because a similar-looking imposter lurks in the forest as well. The false morel is more rust colored, it is not hollow, and its cap hangs free from its stem. The best way to know for sure that the mushroom is a real morel is to cut it in half. Eating a false morel can cause gastrointestinal issues and can even be fatal.

When foraging wild morels, place two fingers at the base of the stalk and pinch it off or slice it off with a knife. This way the underground body of the fungus is not damaged. Young morels should not be harvested because they have not yet released their spores. Foragers usually use mesh bags to collect their bounty.

The first step to prepare morel mushrooms is to rinse them under cold water to remove any grit or bugs. Then slice the mushrooms in half lengthwise and soak them in cold water to remove any remaining particles. Pat the mushrooms dry with paper towels, and then place them in a large skillet with butter and sauté them. Salt and pepper the morels to taste and serve the delicacy atop grilled steaks, pork chops, or chicken parts.

Gathering morels may be a time-consuming process with no guarantees of success, but consider the alternative: at local markets, morels sell for from $30 to $80 a pound!

Spaghetti Squash Primavera

Probably the showiest member of the winter squash family, this squash's flesh, when baked, pulls away from the rind like strands of spaghetti. It is low in calories and rich in nutrients.

2 (2-pound) or 1 (4-pound) spaghetti squash, halved and seeded

5 tablespoons butter, divided

½ sweet onion, like Vidalia, thinly sliced (about 1 cup)

1 cup thinly sliced red bell peppers, cut about 1 inch long

1 teaspoon salt

½ teaspoon black pepper

1 cup grated Parmesan cheese, divided

⅓ cup pine nuts, dry toasted

½ cup snipped fresh flat-leafed parsley

Early in the day: Preheat oven to 350 degrees F. Line a large baking sheet with aluminum foil. Place squash, cut-sides down, on foil. Bake for 1 hour, until squash is cooked through and soft to the touch. Remove from oven and cool for 10 minutes. Using a fork, shred squash into a large bowl.

Meanwhile, melt 3 tablespoons butter in a large nonstick skillet over medium heat. Add onions and sauté, stirring frequently, for 2 minutes. Add bell peppers and sauté, stirring frequently, for 3 minutes more. Add remaining 2 tablespoons butter to skillet during the last 1 minute. Add onion mixture to squash and toss to combine well. Season with salt, pepper, and ½ cup Parmesan cheese. Toss to combine. Add pine nuts and parsley and mix well.

Coat a shallow 10-inch-round baking dish with vegetable cooking spray. Transfer squash mixture to baking dish and sprinkle with remaining ½ cup Parmesan cheese. Cover dish with cling wrap. Refrigerate until needed.

To bake and serve: Preheat oven to 325 degrees F. Bring squash mixture to room temperature. Remove cling wrap and cover baking dish securely with aluminum foil. Bake for 20 minutes, until squash is heated through.

(SERVES 8 TO 10 OR 4 TO 6 WITH LEFTOVERS)

SHUTTERSTOCK

Dramatic rock caves ring Devil's Island, one of the twenty-two Apostle Islands in Lake Superior, off the Bayfield peninsula.
GETTY IMAGES

Side
Shows

Cheesy Baked Hash Browns

These are great potatoes to serve for a large group. The recipe will serve twelve when prepared in a 9 x 13-inch baking dish. I've offered the option to divide the recipe into two portions and freeze half for use at another meal.

1 (30-ounce) package Country Style Hash Brown Shredded Potatoes, thawed

2 cups (1 pint) sour cream

1 (8-ounce) package Sargento Authentic Mexican Artisan Blend shredded cheese

1 cup chopped sweet onions, like Vidalia

3 tablespoons milk

1 teaspoon kosher salt

1 teaspoon cracked black pepper

⅔ cup fresh breadcrumbs

4 tablespoons butter, melted

Preheat oven to 375 degrees F. Mix potatoes, sour cream, shredded cheese, onions, milk, salt, and pepper together in a large bowl. Coat two 8 x 8-inch baking dishes with vegetable cooking spray. Divide potato mixture evenly between the two dishes.

Place breadcrumbs in a medium bowl. Pour melted butter over crumbs and stir with a fork to coat crumbs evenly. Sprinkle the buttered breadcrumbs evenly atop the potato mixture in each dish. Place one dish in the oven and bake, uncovered, for 45 minutes. Cover other dish with cling wrap, then aluminum foil, and freeze until needed. Thaw before baking.

Chef's note: Wisconsin-made Sargento brand Authentic Mexican Artisan Blend shredded cheese is a combination of *queso quesadilla*, *asadero*, *queso gallego*, *manchego*, and *anejo enchilade* cheeses.

(SERVES 12; SERVES 6 IN EACH DISH)

Salt and Vinegar Baby Red Potatoes

Red potatoes have less starch but more sugar than white potatoes. They have a light, creamy flavor, the perfect canvas for salt and vinegar.

1 pound baby red potatoes, cut in half

½ cup plus 1 tablespoon white balsamic vinegar, divided

1½ tablespoons butter

Salt and freshly ground black pepper

Up to 3 hours ahead: Place potatoes and ½ cup vinegar in a medium saucepan. Add water to cover potatoes by an inch. Bring to boil on medium-high heat, then reduce heat to medium and simmer until fork tender, about 10 to 12 minutes. Drain potatoes and pat them dry. Transfer potatoes to a zipper bag. Refrigerate until needed.

To cook and serve: Melt butter in a large skillet over medium-high heat. Add potatoes and season generously with salt and pepper. Cook potatoes, tossing them frequently, until they are golden brown and slightly crispy. Sprinkle with remaining 1 tablespoon of vinegar and toss to combine. Transfer to a serving bowl and serve immediately.

Chef's note: I use freshly ground pink Himalayan kosher salt. You can use simple white vinegar in this recipe if you wish.

(SERVES 4)

German Potato Salad

My favorite aunt, Fern, learned this heirloom recipe from my German grandmother and has preserved it for the ages. The warm bacon dressing with vinegar sets it apart from other versions of potato salad. The flavors get better when they marry for a few days, so this is a great salad to make ahead and reheat.

8 medium (2½-inch diameter) Yukon Gold potatoes, cut in quarters

8 slices bacon, cut into ½-inch pieces

¼ cup flour

1½ cups water

5 tablespoons white vinegar

¾ cup sugar

1 cup chopped celery

¾ cup chopped sweet onions, like Vidalia

Salt and freshly ground black pepper

Place potatoes in a large pot with water to cover. Boil potatoes until cooked through but still firm, about 15 minutes. Drain potatoes; peel and cut them into ¼-inch-thick slices.

While potatoes are boiling, place bacon in a large frying pan over medium heat and fry until crispy. Remove bacon with a slotted spoon and place it on paper toweling to drain. Reserve ¼ cup bacon grease in pan; discard the rest. Stir flour into bacon grease. Add water, vinegar, and sugar. Stir over medium heat until mixture is smooth and sugar is dissolved.

Add celery, onions, and potatoes. Stir to mix well. Season with salt and pepper to taste. Reduce heat to medium-low and simmer, stirring frequently, for 15 minutes.

Chef's note: You can prepare potato salad up to two days ahead. Simmer for only 5 minutes instead of 15. Transfer potato salad to a covered container and refrigerate until needed. Reheat potato salad in a large skillet over medium-low heat for 15 minutes or until heated through.

(SERVES 6)

Wild Rice—The Wondrous Grain

One of the few grains native to the United States, wild rice is actually not rice at all, but a tall aquatic grass with a plume-like top, bearing slender seeds, that grows in shallow lakes and streams in northern Wisconsin and northern Minnesota. Long a staple in the diets of the Ojibwe (Chippewa) tribes inhabiting the area, wild rice is a high-protein, low-fat super food that has a nutty taste and an interesting texture.

According to tribal legend, centuries ago, driven out of the northeast, the Ojibwe were instructed by their Supreme Being to find the place where food grows on water. This led them to the northern inland lakes of the upper Midwest—Wisconsin, Michigan, and Minnesota, where they discovered *manoomin*, "the good berry" or "wonderous grain" that is known in English as wild rice.

Wild rice is harvested in late August and early September, during what the Ojibwe called the "wild rice moon" or "rice making moon." In the autumn, Ojibwe families camped near the wild rice stands, where they harvested the grains by hand from canoes. One person would maneuver the canoe through the wild rice beds, using a long, forked push-pole. A second person would use two ricing sticks or "knockers"—one in each hand—to simultaneously pull the grass over the canoe and knock the ripe rice kernels into the bottom of the canoe. About four-fifths of the seeds would fall back into the water, seeding future crops. (Harvested wild rice looks like large green grass seed.) The seeds were then parched over a wood fire to dry and roast, then thrashed to remove the hulls, and finally cleaned of any hull particles.

Wild rice is not actually rice at all, but rather the slender seeds of aquatic grass.
GETTY IMAGES

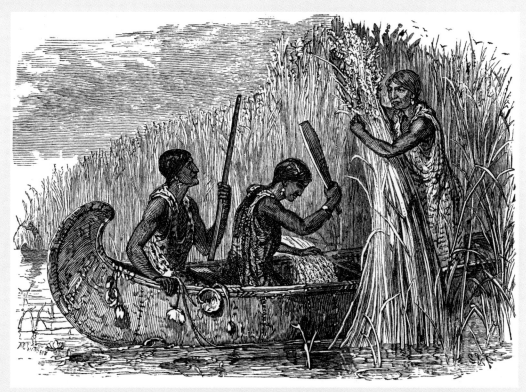

The Ojibwe harvested *manoomin* (wild rice) by hand from canoes. GETTY IMAGES

Real wild rice is still harvested this way today. (It takes two to three pounds of green, unprocessed rice to yield one pound of finished, processed wild rice.) What you see sold in most grocery stores, however, is an imposter of sorts—cultivated rice, farm-grown in a flooded paddy. Paddy-grown wild rice is left wet for at least a week, to soften the hulls, which makes the grains harden and blacken. This process makes the rice tougher and less flavorful and lengthens the cooking time. Real wild rice, however, has a mild, delicate flavor and a tender texture, is a milky brown color, and pops delicately when bitten into.

Once found from Manitoba to Florida, real wild rice harvests have declined dramatically over the last century, limited now to northern Wisconsin and northern Minnesota. But even more significantly, in the last decade, the volume of wild rice dropped from 5,000 acres to less than 1,000 acres across forty bodies of Wisconsin waters. Local ricers attribute the decline to everything from climate change (too much or too little rain), to logging, shoreline development and lawn fertilizer, to invasive plants and fish.

Harvesting of wild rice is allowed on some designated public lakes and waterways in northern Wisconsin with possession of a wild rice harvest permit, during a date-regulated harvest season. Contact the Wisconsin Department of Natural Resources (DNR) for more information: dnr.wisconsin.gov. Typically, only tribal members can harvest wild rice within Native American reservations.

Wild rice terminology is confusing: The plant is called wild rice whether it is paddy-raised or grows in the wild. To identify their product as truly wild, many harvesters are labeling their product with the Ojibwe word, *manoomin*. You can purchase "real" wild rice online at: nativeharvest.com.

Cranberry Wild Rice

1 cup "real" wild rice (*manoomin*)

4 cups water

½ teaspoon salt

1½ tablespoons butter

1 cup finely chopped white button mushrooms

½ cup chopped sweet onions, like Vidalia

⅓ cup finely chopped celery

1 cup sweetened dried cranberries, rehydrated in water and drained

Salt and freshly ground black pepper

Wash wild rice in 3 changes of hot tap water. Place rice, water, and salt in a medium-large saucepan over medium-high heat. (Cooked rice will triple in volume.) Bring to a boil. Reduce heat to low and cover. Simmer until wild rice has absorbed the water, 30 to 50 minutes. (Wild rice may have different preparation times. Light colored rice takes less time to cook than dark colored rice.) Fluff rice with a fork. Wild rice should be tender, cracked and curled, but not mushy).

Meanwhile, while rice is cooking, melt butter in a large nonstick skillet over medium heat. Add mushrooms, onions, celery, and cranberries. Sauté, stirring frequently, for 5 minutes, until onions are soft and mushroom liquid has evaporated. Toss vegetables with rice. Season with salt and pepper to taste. Serve immediately.

Chef's note: You can substitute sweetened dried apricots, cherries, or mango for the cranberries in this recipe.

(SERVES 8 TO 10)

Wava's Foolproof Scalloped Potatoes

My longtime Wisconsin-born friend Wava says you can't miss with these potatoes, and they are a "very, very yummy" family favorite.

1 tablespoon butter plus ¼ cup melted butter

4 cups peeled and thinly sliced Yukon Gold potatoes

1 cup finely diced ham

1½ cups milk

1¼ teaspoons salt

4 tablespoons flour

¼ cup chopped onions

Preheat oven to 350 degrees F. Use 1 tablespoon butter to coat a 9 x 13-inch baking dish. Layer potatoes in dish. Sprinkle 1 cup finely diced ham over potatoes. Place melted butter, milk, salt, flour, and onions in a blender and blend until smooth. Pour mixture over potatoes.

Cover dish with aluminum foil and bake for 30 minutes. Remove foil and bake uncovered for another 60 minutes, until potatoes are a nice golden color. Serve immediately.

(SERVES 4 TO 6)

Twice-Baked Stuffed Potatoes

Serve these savory potatoes as a main course, just as they are, or top them with chili, taco meat, or shredded chicken.

3 Idaho baking potatoes (about 1 pound), washed and dried

Olive oil spray

¾ teaspoon salt, plus more for sprinkling

5 tablespoons butter, softened

½ cup sour cream

3 egg yolks

1 tablespoon snipped fresh chives

½ teaspoon black pepper

6 heaping tablespoons shredded sharp cheddar cheese

Up to one day ahead: Preheat oven to 375 degrees F. Coat all surfaces of potatoes with olive oil spray and sprinkle lightly with salt. Place potatoes directly on the lower oven rack and bake for 1 to 1¼ hours, until potatoes can be easily pierced with a fork.

Cut potatoes in half lengthwise. Carefully scoop out pulp with a small spoon and place it in a large bowl. Set potato shells aside. Cut butter into 5 pieces and add to hot potatoes. Mash butter into potatoes with a fork.

Whisk sour cream, egg yolks, chives, remaining ¾ teaspoon salt, and black pepper together in a small bowl. Mash mixture into potatoes with a fork, until well combined. Spoon mashed potato mixture into potato shells. Top each potato with a heaping tablespoon of shredded cheese. Place in a large shallow covered container and refrigerate until needed.

To bake: Preheat oven to 350 degrees F. Bring stuffed potatoes to room temperature. Place potatoes in a large baking dish or on a baking sheet. Bake potatoes, uncovered, for 45 minutes or until heated through.

(SERVES 6)

DAIRY FARMERS OF WISCONSIN

Parmesan Risotto with Ham, Baby Spinach, and Slivered Tomatoes

A basic risotto has five components: broth (chicken, vegetable, beef, seafood), aromatics (onions, garlic, shallots, celery, carrots), fat (butter, oil, bacon grease), Arborio rice, and enhancements (cheese, seafood, vegetables, meats). Follow the simple technique described in this recipe and create a new risotto every time, just by varying ingredients. Risotto takes just 20 minutes, from the first addition of broth to the finish.

1 (48-ounce) carton low sodium chicken broth

4 tablespoons butter, divided

1 cup finely chopped sweet onions, like Vidalia

1 teaspoon garlic paste or minced garlic

2 cups Arborio rice

½ cup white wine

½ cup Parmesan cheese

½ cup thin-sliced delicatessen honey ham, cut into ¼-inch-wide strips

3 cups chopped baby spinach

1 cup quartered grape tomatoes

2 tablespoons snipped parsley

Bring broth to simmer in a medium saucepan over medium-low heat. Reduce heat to low and keep broth at a simmer.

Melt 2 tablespoons butter in a large nonstick saucepan over medium heat. Add onions and garlic and sauté for 1½ minutes, stirring frequently, until onions are soft. Add rice and sauté, stirring constantly, for 1½ minutes, until edges of rice are transparent and centers are still white.

Add wine and stir until absorbed, about 1 minute. Add 1 cup warm broth and cook until liquid is absorbed but rice is not dry, stirring every 1 to 2 minutes. Repeat process, adding 3 more cups broth, one cup at a time, and stirring frequently until broth is absorbed. Then add remaining broth, ½ cup at a time, stirring frequently until liquid is absorbed. (Taste a kernel of rice between each addition of broth at this point to check consistency.)

When rice is tender on the outside but still al dente in the center, remove from heat. (Rice should be creamy, not soupy or dry, with a toothy center.) Cut remaining 2 tablespoons butter into small pieces. Stir butter and Parmesan cheese into risotto. Stir in ham, spinach, and tomatoes. Serve immediately. Sprinkle each serving with parsley.

(SERVES 4 TO 6)

Wisconsin Emmentaler Swiss Cheese

Emmentaler is the original Swiss cheese, first produced more than eight centuries ago in the alpine valley of Switzerland's Emme River. Three types of Swiss cheese are presently made in Wisconsin—Wisconsin Swiss, Baby Swiss, and Emmentaler. Holed and rindless, Wisconsin Swiss is buttery and slightly sweet. A great melting cheese, Baby Swiss uses whole milk and is produced in smaller wheels. Mild and creamy, it is aged for less time than Wisconsin Swiss (usually a month), and it has smaller holes.

Emmentaler has a rich, nutty, buttery, slightly fruity flavor, a smooth texture, and large holes. Only one Wisconsin artisan cheese factory—Edelweiss Creamery—makes Emmentaler in the Old World Swiss way, in a copper kettle. Bruce Workman, Master Cheesemaker and owner of Edelweiss Creamery, procured an old-fashioned copper kettle from Switzerland, in which he produces his Emmentaler in 180-pound wheels.

From milk to wheel, it takes four and a half hours, Workman says. The copper kettle is special because it heats up evenly and imparts flavor when the milk and curds are stirred around, he further states. When removed from the kettle, the cheese sits in the wheel press for twenty-four hours, then goes into a brine for forty-eight hours, and finally is transferred to the cold room for a week, where, Workman says, the formation of the holes in the cheese will even out. From the cold room, the cheese wheel goes to the aging room, where it is flipped and hand-washed with a saltwater solution multiple times a week for two months before it is cut and packaged.

DAIRY FARMERS OF WISCONSIN

Emmentaler Cheese Bread

½ cup butter, softened

2 tablespoons mayonnaise

1 tablespoon Dijon mustard

1 tablespoon lemon juice

2 teaspoons dried onion flakes

1 loaf Italian bread

1¼ cups shredded Emmentaler Swiss cheese

Preheat oven to 375 degrees F. Place butter, mayonnaise, mustard, lemon juice, and onion flakes in a small bowl. Stir to mix well.

Slice bread into 1-inch-thick pieces. Spread butter mixture on one side of each bread slice, then sprinkle with cheese and press it into the butter. Reassemble the slices into a loaf, buttered side against unbuttered side. Place loaf on a double piece of aluminum foil on a baking sheet. Bend foil around lower loaf to hold slices in place but don't completely encase the bread in foil.

Place bread in preheated oven and bake, uncovered, for 10 to 15 minutes, until the cheese is melted and the bread crust is crisp.

(SERVES 8)

Sweet Finales

Babycakes

Babycakes are the ultimate make-ahead dessert. These individual cakes, baked in maxi-muffin pans, are frozen until needed, then defrosted on dessert plates for a mere 30 minutes.

Classic Carrot Babycakes

3 cups flour

2 teaspoons baking soda

¼ teaspoon salt

1 teaspoon cinnamon

3 large eggs

2 cups sugar

1½ cups canola oil

3 teaspoons vanilla, divided

1 (16-ounce) can crushed pineapple with juices

2 cups grated raw carrots

1 cup finely chopped walnuts

1 (1-pound) box confectioners' sugar

¼ cup butter, softened at room temperature

1 (8-ounce) package cream cheese, softened at room temperature

Up to 1 month ahead: Preheat oven to 350 degrees F. Sift together flour, baking soda, salt, and cinnamon. Set aside. Beat eggs in the large bowl of an electric mixer. Add sugar and beat until well combined. Add oil and beat until frothy.

Add flour mixture, several tablespoons at a time, beating on medium speed and scraping down bowl often. Add 1 teaspoon vanilla, pineapple, carrots, and walnuts. Beat on low speed until well combined.

Place paper liners in cups of 2 (6-count) maxi-muffin pans. Spoon batter into paper liners, filling them about three-quarters full. Bake for 30 minutes or until an inserted wooden skewer comes out clean. (Repeat with remaining batter.)

While cakes are baking, make the cream cheese frosting. Place confectioners' sugar, butter, cream cheese, and remaining 2 teaspoons vanilla in the large bowl of an electric mixer. Beat until creamy.

Remove cakes from oven. Pulling gently on the paper liners, remove cakes from muffin pans and allow them to cool on a wire rack for 5 minutes. Remove paper liners from cakes and transfer cakes to parchment- or waxed-paper-lined baking sheets. Cool for 10 minutes more.

Frost tops and sides of each babycake with cream cheese frosting. Place baking sheets in freezer and freeze cakes until firm, about 2 hours. Transfer cakes to large parchment- or waxed-paper-lined covered containers. Freeze cakes until needed.

Thirty minutes before serving: Place individual cakes on dessert plates and allow them to defrost.

(MAKES 15 BABYCAKES)

Cherry-Fudge Babycakes

1 (18.25-ounce) package chocolate-fudge cake mix

1 (21-ounce) can cherry pie filling

3 large eggs

1 teaspoon almond extract

5 tablespoons butter

1 cup sugar

⅓ cup milk

1 cup semisweet chocolate chips

Ice cream, for serving

Preheat oven to 350 degrees F. Place paper liners in maxi-muffin cups. Place cake mix, pie filling, eggs, and almond extract in the bowl of an electric mixer. Beat until well blended, about 2 minutes. Spoon batter into paper liners, filling a little more than half full. Bake for 17 minutes or until an inserted wooden skewer comes out clean.

Meanwhile, while cakes are baking, prepare frosting. Melt butter in a small saucepan over medium heat. Add sugar and milk. Bring to a boil, stirring constantly, for 1 minute. Remove frosting from heat. Stir in chocolate chips until melted and smooth.

Remove cakes from oven. Pulling gently on the paper liners, remove cakes from pan and cool on a wire rack for 2 minutes. Remove paper liners from cakes and transfer them to a parchment or waxed-paper-lined baking sheet.

Using a spoon, drizzle frosting onto cakes, completely covering tops and allowing frosting to run down the sides and pool on the paper. Using a table knife, spread the pooled frosting up the sides of the cakes. (If frosting gets too hard to run down sides of cakes, reheat for a few seconds.)

Using a firm spatula, transfer frosted cakes to 2 parchment- or waxed-paper-lined large, covered containers. Freeze babycakes until needed. To serve: Defrost each cake on an individual dessert plate for about 20 minutes. Serve with a scoop of ice cream on the side.

Chef's note: You'll need two 6-count (6-inch, 8-ounce) maxi-muffin pans and paper liners for this recipe. You can find them in stores that sell kitchen supplies. A good addition to any cook's stash of equipment, they are extremely versatile for baking both sweet and savory individual dishes.

(MAKES 12 BABYCAKES)

Death by Chocolate Mousse Trifle

This dessert requires a little plan-ahead time to put together, but the rewards for your efforts are tenfold. Not only is the presentation elegantly beautiful, the dessert itself is lip-smacking good. And the bonus is that you can spoon leftover trifle into a fresh serving bowl, swirl the top with a spoon, cover and freeze it for another time. Simply defrost it in the refrigerator and serve. It's even better the second time around.

1 (17-ounce) package frozen Duncan Hines Oven Ready Homestyle Brownies

⅓ cup Bailey's Irish Crème

6 large Heath bars

1 cup water

1 (3.1-ounce) package Dr. Oetker Mousse Supreme, Dark Chocolate Truffle flavor

1 (8-ounce) container Cool Whip, thawed

One to two days ahead: Preheat oven to 350 degrees F. Bake brownies for 25 minutes, until cooked through but not hardened. Pour Bailey's over hot brownies. Allow to cool. Cover with foil and keep at room temperature for at least one day, until ready to assemble trifle.

Early in the day or before dinner: To assemble trifle, break up Heath bars and place in the bowl of a food processor. Pulse until Heath bars are evenly crushed.

Place water in the bowl of an electric mixer. Add mousse mix and beat on slow speed until slightly thickened, about 30 seconds. Increase speed to high and beat for 3 to 5 minutes, until fluffy.

Break up brownies into bite-size pieces and place in a shallow glass bowl, lining the bottom and sides. Sprinkle half the crushed Heath bars over the brownies. Spread mousse over brownies. Top with a layer of Cool Whip. Sprinkle remaining crushed Heath bars over trifle. Refrigerate until needed. (To make individual trifles: Layer trifle, as listed above, into long-stemmed bubble wine glasses or stemless red wine glasses.)

Chef's note: The brownies need to be prepared at least one day ahead of time, so that the flavor of the Bailey's marries with the chocolate. If you prefer, you can bake a packaged brownie mix instead of the freezer-ready brownies. It will add a few minutes time, but you'll only have to use half the brownies for this dessert. If you don't have Bailey's, substitute Kahlua instead. Dr. Oetker brand mousse is superior but if you can't find it, substitute Jell-O No Bake Chocolate Mousse.

(SERVES 12)

English Trifle

An authentic English trifle is always made with Bird's Custard powder, not always easy to find in the United States. If you want to use it instead of the Jell-O Americana custard called for in this recipe, you can order it on Amazon.

1 (3-ounce) package wild strawberry Jell-O

1 cup boiling water

1 cup pineapple juice

2 (3-ounce) packages ladyfingers

½ cup raspberry jam

1 (1-pound) package frozen sliced peaches, thawed, drained, and diced (about 2 cups)

4 cups thinly sliced strawberries

2 cups blueberries

2 tablespoons cream sherry

1 (2.9-ounce) package Jell-O Americana custard

2 cups whole milk or 1 cup half-and-half and 1 cup skim milk

1 (8-ounce) carton heavy whipping cream

2 teaspoons confectioners' sugar

⅓ cup sliced almonds, dry toasted

One day ahead: Place strawberry Jell-O powder in a medium bowl. Pour boiling water over powder and stir until dissolved. Stir in pineapple juice. Set aside to cool.

Meanwhile, separate ladyfingers. Spread the flat side of each ladyfinger with raspberry jam. Line the sides of a large glass punch bowl or trifle bowl with ladyfingers, jam-side in. Place a triple layer of ladyfingers in a crisscross pattern in the bottom of the bowl, jam-side up.

Place peaches atop ladyfingers in an even layer. Place strawberries in an even layer atop peaches. Place blueberries atop strawberries. Sprinkle sherry atop fruit. Pour cooled Jello-O over fruit, allowing it to seep down into the ladyfinger layers. With the back of a large spoon, press on fruit, compressing the layers. Cover with cling wrap and refrigerate until Jell-O is set, about 1 hour.

Meanwhile, place custard powder in a medium nonstick saucepan. Whisk in milk and place saucepan over medium heat. Whisking constantly, cook custard until it comes to a full boil, about 5 minutes. Transfer custard to a medium bowl and place a sheet of cling wrap directly on top of custard so that no film will form. Set aside and allow custard to cool to room temperature, 30 to 45 minutes.

When custard has cooled so that it is not yet set but won't melt the Jell-O, spoon it atop trifle. Cover bowl with cling wrap and refrigerate until ready to serve.

Place whipping cream in the large bowl of an electric mixer. Beat on high until cream starts to thicken. Add sugar and continue beating until stiff peaks form. Transfer to a covered container and refrigerate until needed.

Up to 1 hour ahead: Spread whipped cream atop trifle, sprinkle with almonds, cover with cling wrap, and refrigerate until serving.

Chef's note: You can make many creative substitutions in this recipe: use any in-season fruit in the same proportions; 2 teaspoons almond or banana extract for the sherry; half an angel food or pound cake for the ladyfingers; Cool Whip for the whipping cream.

(SERVES 12 TO 15)

Into the Sugarbush

Centuries ago, the Ojibwe of northern Wisconsin annually harvested sap from the sugar maple forests. As winter turned into spring, the tribes would go to "sugar camp," setting up wigwams in the maple groves (sugarbushes), where they tapped the trees, collected the sap in birchbark containers, and turned it into syrup and sugar. Day and night, they boiled the sap in big kettles over an open fire, reducing it to a thick syrup. (Sometimes the children poured the maple syrup into the snow, making a taffy-like candy.)

To make sugar, the Ojibwe strained the syrup, put it back in the kettles, and reduced it further, then put it in troughs, where, with a paddle, they worked it until it was granulated. This hard sugar was placed in birchbark cones for storage. As the Ojibwe had no salt, they seasoned everything from fruits and vegetables to fish and meat with maple sugar.

European settlers continued the maple sugaring tradition and today, commercial and family-run sugarbushes pepper the state, which ranks fourth in nationwide maple syrup production (300,000 gallons in 2021). The ideal time for tapping the maple is when temperatures are in the forties during the day but just below freezing at night, a period of about a month. This temperature change causes the tree to swell and contract, pumping the sap throughout the tree and out any open wounds (like the inserted tap).

Four types of maple trees can be tapped for their sap—sugar, silver, red, and black—but sugar maple sap has the highest sugar content. A tree must be at least ten inches in diameter to be successfully tapped, because the sap is found in the tree's third layer. A 1½- to 2-inch hole is tapped into the tree and a spigot is attached to it. A bucket hanging from the spigot collects the sap. It takes forty gallons of sap to make one gallon of syrup.

Commercial operations today, such as those at Maple Hollow Syrup, are much more sophisticated. There, the sap is gently drawn out with a vacuum line and sent to the pumping station, which has sensory controls to turn the system off at night when the temperature drops. From the pumping station, it goes to large stainless tanks in the syrup house for cooking. Through reverse osmosis, two-thirds of the water is extracted, and gravitational pull takes the sap concentrate to a wood-fired evaporator for cooking. Then it is streamed through filter presses and stored in drums. Before bottling, the syrup is heated and filtered again.

Among the family-owned maple sugar producers Up North for generations are Maple Hollow Syrup, Merrill (maplehollowsyrup.com); Anderson's Maple Syrup, Cumberland (andersonsmaplesyrup.com); Midwest Maple Syrup, Phillips (midwestmaple.com); Hustad's Sugar Bush, Cumberland (hustadsmaplesyrup.com); Glenna Farms, Amery (glennafarms.com); Z-Orchard, Amery (z-orchard.com); Morley's Maple Syrup, Luck (morleysmaplesyrup.com).

Maple Bacon Crack

The Holoubek family has been maple sugaring for four generations. Today their company, Midwest Maple, collects sap from 2,900 taps over 17 acres in Phillips, in northern Wisconsin. They shared their family recipe for this wildly decadent, sugary, maple bacon snack. They use it for a side at breakfast, but it could be eaten any time of the day. I can see why they named it Maple Bacon Crack. It's highly addictive!

10 slices bacon, thinly sliced

1 (8-ounce) package Pillsbury Crescent Dough Sheet

4 ounces (½ cup) maple syrup, divided

¾ cup brown sugar

Preheat oven to 375 degrees F. Line a baking sheet with parchment paper. Spray it with olive oil spray and brush it over the paper so that the paper is evenly coated with oil.

In a large skillet over medium-high heat, cook bacon until crispy. Remove bacon with a slotted spoon and drain on a paper towel-lined plate.

Roll out crescent dough sheet onto the parchment paper. Press with your fingertips to make an even rectangle. Prick the dough all over with a fork. Drizzle 2 ounces of maple syrup over dough. Brush syrup so that the dough is evenly coated. Top with brown sugar, making sure it is evenly distributed and doing your best to cover the dough completely. Top with cooked bacon, distributing it evenly. Drizzle remaining 2 ounces maple syrup atop bacon.

Bake 20 to 22 minutes, until golden. Cool completely before slicing into pieces and serving.

(MAKES 15 3-INCH SQUARES)

MIDWEST MAPLE

Make-Ahead Fresh Peach Pie

The sweet, unadulterated flavor of fresh peaches shines through in this easy, make-ahead pie. Take advantage of fresh peach season by freezing filling for multiple pies, which you can enjoy all year long.

1½ cups sugar

2 tablespoons cornstarch

3 tablespoons Minute Tapioca

9 to 10 fresh free-stone peaches
(6 cups sliced)

1 (15-ounce) package rolled
Pillsbury Pie Crusts (2 crusts)

Up to 3 months ahead: Mix sugar, cornstarch, and tapioca together in a medium bowl. Set aside.

Bring a medium saucepan of water to boil over high heat. Remove pan from heat and place on a hot pad. Place each peach in hot water for about 30 seconds. Remove peaches from water and peel each one. Slice each peach and put slices in a large bowl. Add sugar mixture and toss until peaches are well coated.

Place two large pieces of aluminum foil inside a 10-inch-diameter aluminum pie pan, pressing so that foil conforms to pie pan. Transfer peach mixture to pie pan. Cover with a double layer of foil and crimp edges securely. Freeze until needed.

To bake: Preheat oven to 450 degrees F. Remove pie pan from freezer and remove foil-lined peach filling from pan. Roll out 1 pie crust to fit the 10-inch-diameter pie pan. Trim bottom crust around pan edge. Remove all foil from peach filling and place frozen filling into pie crust. Roll out second crust and place atop filling. Wrap excess crust under edge of bottom crust. Crimp edges. Cut 4 or 5 slits in the top crust.

Place pie on a baking sheet. Cut aluminum foil into 2-inch strips. Place strips around edges of crust to form a protective collar. (This will keep edges from overcooking.) Bake for 20 minutes. Reduce heat to 350 degrees F and bake for 50 minutes more. Remove foil collars from crust and bake 25 to 30 minutes longer, until pie is bubbly and crust is golden. Allow to cool for at least 15 minutes before serving.

Chef's note: Substitute an equal amount of fresh sliced strawberries, blueberries, blackberries, or peeled, cored, sliced apples for the peaches whenever these fruits are in season.

(SERVES 8)

The Way Up North Fruit Loop

Bayfield, on the shores of the westernmost edge of Lake Superior, enjoys a unique microclimate that allows a panoply of berry farms and apple orchards to flourish in the northernmost reach of Wisconsin. Known as the Berry Capital of Wisconsin, the fruit industry in Bayfield began in 1905, when William Knight planted the first commercial orchard in the area. He planted twenty acres of cherries and twenty acres of apples. The next year, he planted thousands more. (Some of the original trees, now a part of Hauser's Superior View Farm, are still producing apples.)

Today, more than a dozen farms and orchards pepper the Bayfield countryside, all within a few-mile radius of each other. Farm stands, orchard shops, and the Saturday local farmers' market offer the season's bounty for sale. Strawberries generally start becoming ripe at the end of June. July and August see an abundance of currants, juneberries, sweet and tart cherries, raspberries, gooseberries, then blueberries and blackberries. As the weather starts to cool, grapes, pears, plums, and apples of every variety come into season. Visitors can meander the backroads of the hilly surrounds of Bayfield in a self-guided tour the Chamber of Commerce calls "the Fruit Loop."

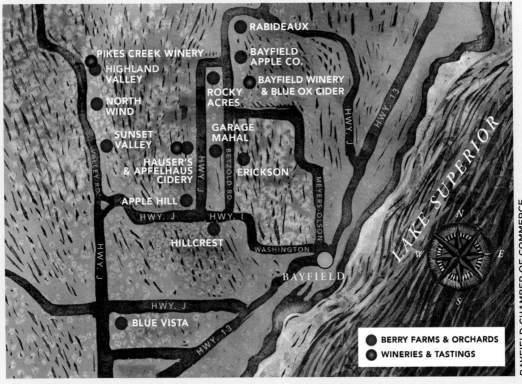

BAYFIELD CHAMBER OF COMMERCE

The aforementioned Hauser's Superior View Farm, a five-generation operation that includes a greenhouse, nursery, orchard, and cidery, was founded in 1908 by a Swiss horticulturist named John F. Hauser, who grew strawberries and potatoes. When his son took over the farm, he planted orchards, growing apples and pears. Over the ensuing decades, the ever-expanding farm was passed down from father to son. Hauser's sits 600 feet above and two and a half miles from Lake Superior and the picturesque Apostle Islands, offering what their name promises, a "Superior" view.

Bayfield Apple Company, a tree fruit and berry orchard, is open to the public year-round. Visitors are welcome to explore the property and experience seasonal happenings, such as apples being pressed for cider or watching jam being made. Bayfield grows twenty-four varieties of apples as well as pears, cherries, currants, and blueberries. They also have the largest raspberry crop in Wisconsin.

Located on a remote, wooded peninsula, Blue Vista Farm overlooks Lake Superior. Named for the surrounding water and blue skies, the sustainable farm has planted six acres of blueberries, five acres of raspberries, and 1,500 apple trees since they took over the land in 1988.

Besides the three establishments described above, the farms, orchards, and wineries of the Fruit Loop include: Weber Orchards, Hillcrest Orchard, Apple Hill Orchard, Sunset Valley Orchard, North Wind Organic Farm, Good Earth Gardens, Highland Valley Farm, Pike's Creek Winery, Rocky Acres Berry Farm, Garage Mahal Orchard, Erickson's Orchard, Bayfield Winery and Blue Ox Cider, and Rabideaux's Orchard.

Pumpkin Satin Cheesecake Pic

Mommsen's Harvest Hills Pumpkin Patch in Rice Lake is worth a visit in the autumn—pumpkins as far as the eye can see. This variation of classic pumpkin pie is light and airy and easy to make and serve.

1 (8-ounce) package cream cheese, softened

2 tablespoons plus 1 cup milk, divided

2 tablespoons sugar

1 (8-ounce) container Cool Whip at refrigerator temperature

1 (15-ounce) can pumpkin pie filling

2 (3.4-ounce) packages vanilla instant pudding mix

1 teaspoon cinnamon

½ teaspoon ground ginger

¼ teaspoon ground cloves

2 (6-ounce) prepared graham cracker pie crusts

Place cream cheese, 2 tablespoons milk, and sugar in a medium bowl. Beat with an electric mixer until creamy. Whisk in Cool Whip and set aside. In another medium bowl, mix together pumpkin, remaining 1 cup milk, pudding mix, cinnamon, ginger, and cloves. Divide sour cream/whipped topping mixture equally between two pie crusts. Then layer each pie with half the pumpkin mixture. Cover with the inverted plastic lids from prepared pie crusts and refrigerate at least 4 hours or overnight. (Serve pies directly from refrigerator so that Cool Whip layer remains firm.)

(SERVES 12)

Family Heirloom Christmas Sugar Cookies

A closely guarded family secret until now, this recipe has been our Christmas cookie go-to for several generations. Frosting the cookies is a family affair and develops into quite a creativity competition.

FOR THE COOKIES:

1 cup butter, room temperature

1½ cups sugar

2 large eggs, well beaten

1 teaspoon vanilla

3¾ cups flour

1 teaspoon salt

4 teaspoons baking powder

2 tablespoons milk, divided

FOR THE FROSTING:

½ cup (1 stick) butter, softened

3¾ cups confectioners' sugar

3 to 4 tablespoons milk

1 teaspoon vanilla

Assorted food coloring

Sprinkles, candies, and other nonpareils

Two days ahead: To prepare the cookies, with an electric mixer, cream together butter and sugar. Beat in eggs and vanilla. In a separate bowl, sift together flour, salt, and baking powder. Add half the dry ingredients to the butter mixture, several tablespoons at a time, along with 1 tablespoon of milk. Beat until combined, scraping down the bowl several times. Repeat with remaining flour mixture and remaining 1 tablespoon of milk. Transfer to a covered container and refrigerate overnight.

One day ahead: To bake and decorate, preheat oven to 350 degrees F. Roll out dough on a floured board and cut with cookie cutters of your choice (stars, Christmas trees, bells, Santa Claus, angels, etc.). Bake on a greased nonstick baking sheet until light brown, about 10 minutes. Cool on a wire rack. When cool, place in a covered container, layers separated by waxed paper.

To make the frosting: Beat butter with an electric mixer until creamy, about 2 minutes on medium speed. Reduce speed to low and add sugar, ½ cup at a time. Add milk and vanilla and beat on medium speed, 1 to 2 minutes more. Add more milk if necessary to reach the desired spreading consistency.

To frost the cookies: Divide frosting among 5 small bowls and add food coloring so that you have red, green, blue, yellow, and 1 uncolored, white. Assemble sprinkles, candies, and other nonpareils. Frost and decorate cookies. Your only limit is your imagination.

Chef's note: I usually make these cookies over a 3-day period—dough, bake, decorate, because I usually double the dough recipe, and it is a lot of work, but worth the effort, my family says! The recipe makes several dozen, depending upon how large your cookie cutters are.

(MAKES A BUNCH)

Vegan Chocolate Peppermint Crinkle Cookies

Eighteen-year-old Katelyn Hawker won the Best Cookie award and was the Grand Prize Winner of the Toledo Blade Cookie and Candy Contest in 2020 with this recipe. She is presently attending Johnson & Wales University pursuing a culinary degree. After happily spending summer vacations Up North with her grandmother, a longtime friend of mine, Katelyn graciously contributed her award-winning recipe for this book.

1 cup granulated sugar

⅓ cup canola oil

1 tablespoon ground flax seeds

⅓ cup nondairy milk

1 teaspoon pure vanilla extract

½ teaspoon peppermint extract

1¼ cups all-purpose flour

½ cup cocoa powder

1 teaspoon baking powder

¼ teaspoon salt

1 cup confectioners' sugar, for rolling

⅓ cup crushed peppermint candies

Preheat oven to 350 degrees F. Line two baking sheets with parchment paper. In a large bowl, add the sugar and canola oil. Stir with a wooden spoon until well combined and smooth. Add the ground flax seeds, nondairy milk, and vanilla and peppermint extracts; mix well to combine.

Sift in the flour, cocoa powder, baking powder, and salt, using either a sifter or a fine mesh strainer. Stir until combined with the wet ingredients and a soft dough is formed.

Place the confectioners' sugar in a small mixing bowl. Scoop out two tablespoons of dough at a time and shape into a ball. Roll the ball in the sugar very generously, covering all sides. (The more confectioners' sugar, the prettier the cookies will be.)

Place the balls onto the prepared baking sheet, about 2 inches apart so they have room to spread. Bake for 10 to 12 minutes until set. They will appear slightly undercooked and soft, but they will firm up as they cool. Add a pinch of crushed peppermint candies on the top of the cookies.

Cool cookies on the baking sheet for at least 10 minutes, then transfer them to a wire rack. Store cookies in an airtight container.

KATELYN HAWKER

Over-the-Top Ice Cream Sauces

When your sweet tooth calls for ice cream, here is the answer. Whether you prefer a banana split or an ice cream sundae, you'll be sure to love these homemade sauces. Choose hot fudge, butterscotch, or mixed berry sauce—or all three—and create your own masterpiece.

Hot Fudge Sauce

½ cup butter, cut into 8 tablespoons

6 (1-ounce) squares unsweetened chocolate

1 cup evaporated milk

2½ cups confectioners' sugar

1 teaspoon vanilla

Place about 3 inches water in the bottom of a double boiler. Place butter and chocolate in top of double boiler. Place double boiler over high heat, covered, and melt butter and chocolate, stirring frequently, about 10 minutes. When both are melted, reduce heat to medium-low and add evaporated milk and sugar. Stir to combine and cook for 5 minutes, stirring constantly, until sugar is melted and sauce is smooth. Remove pan from heat and stir in vanilla. Transfer to a covered container and refrigerate until needed. Warm sauce in microwave for 30 to 45 seconds before serving or serve hot fudge sauce at room temperature.

(MAKES 3 CUPS)

LIFE IS FULL OF HARD CHOICES

GET A SCOOP OF EACH

DAIRY FARMERS OF WISCONSIN

Butterscotch Sauce

3 tablespoons butter

¼ cup light corn syrup

⅔ cup light brown sugar, firmly packed

Pinch salt

⅓ cup evaporated milk

Pinch baking soda

1 teaspoon vanilla

Place butter, corn syrup, brown sugar, and salt in a medium saucepan over medium heat. Cook, stirring frequently, until butter is melted and sugar is dissolved, about 2½ minutes. When mixture comes to a boil, reduce heat to low, and simmer for 2 minutes, stirring occasionally. Meanwhile, mix evaporated milk, baking soda, and vanilla together in a small bowl. Add milk mixture and cook for 1½ minutes more, stirring constantly, until sauce is smooth and well mixed. Remove pan from heat and allow sauce to cool for 5 minutes. Transfer to a covered container and refrigerate until needed. Warm sauce in microwave for 30 to 45 seconds before serving.

(MAKES 1 CUP)

All Berry Sauce

1 (16-ounce) package frozen mixed berries

⅓ cup dark brown sugar, firmly packed

2 tablespoons fresh lemon juice

2 tablespoons crème de cassis (black currant liqueur) or blackberry syrup (optional)

Dash of cinnamon

Place frozen berries, brown sugar, lemon juice, and liqueur in a medium saucepan over medium heat. Stir to combine, and cook mixture for 4 minutes, stirring frequently, until sugar dissolves and berries soften. Reduce heat to medium-low and simmer for 6 minutes, stirring occasionally. Remove from heat and cool for 5 minutes. Transfer to a covered container and refrigerate until needed. Warm sauce in microwave for 30 to 45 seconds before serving, or serve sauce cold or at room temperature.

(MAKES 2 CUPS)

Ice Cream Drinks—the Boozy Dessert

Wisconsin being the "Dairy State," it's little wonder that its bartenders would concoct a unique bunch of cocktails incorporating ice cream. These boozy ice cream drinks have been around since the nineteenth century, when James Tufts of Racine, Wisconsin, invented a hand-cranked ice cream mixer. His original test cocktail included milk, ice, flavored syrup, and a dash of port. By 1892, bartender William Schmidt was making more than twenty different ice cream cocktails with the invention, such as the Glorious Fourth, a decadent mixture of vanilla ice cream, brandy, and Jamaican rum.

The boozy drinks' popularity continued into the twentieth century. In 1922, Stephen Poplawski, also of Racine, developed the first electric blender. He wired small, spinning blades to a small electric motor and attached the blades to a specially molded clear glass container. It took him more than ten years to patent it. Fred Osius, a Wisconsin resident, along with his two key associates, Louis Hamilton and Chester Beach, acquired the rights to mass-produce Poplawski's blender. They modified the design, creating a form-fitting top for the glass container. By the 1950s, Hamilton-Beach blenders were commonplace in homes across America.

So, it's serendipitous that the Wisconsin-invented blender met Wisconsin ice cream in such a delicious marriage. And since Wisconsin has always had a love affair with after-dinner cocktails, it didn't take long for the threesome to become a firm enduring tradition in supper clubs across the state. Besides the classic ice cream drinks like the Brandy Alexander, Pink Squirrel, and Grasshopper, bartenders use their endless imaginations to create new unique concoctions.

Bryant Sharp opened a cocktail lounge back in 1938 in Milwaukee, Wisconsin, in a Miller Brewing "tied house," where he invented the famous Pink Squirrel drink. He is also credited with inventing the Banana Banshee and the Blue Tail Fly, featured below.

Banana Banshee

1.25 ounces crème de cocoa

1.25 ounces crème de banana

2 large scoops vanilla ice cream

One ripe banana, cut into pieces

Place all ingredients in a blender. Blend until creamy.

(SERVES 1)

Blue Tail Fly

1 ounce blue Curaçao

1 ounce white crème de cacao

3 large scoops vanilla ice cream

Place Curaçao and crème de cacao in a blender with 2 scoops ice cream. Blend until smooth. Add the remaining scoop of ice cream until mixture has a milkshake consistency.

(SERVES 1)

Drunken Strawberries with Almond Whipped Cream

Up North pick-your-own strawberry farms, such as Rocky Acres in Bayfield, Golden Eagle in Lac Du Flambeau, and Basket Flats in Marengo note that strawberry season is from mid-June to early July.

1 quart strawberries

½ cup sugar

½ cup Cointreau or Grand Marnier

3 tablespoons sliced almonds

1 cup whipping cream

2 tablespoons confectioners' sugar

1 teaspoon almond extract

One hour ahead: Slice strawberries and place them in a medium container. Add sugar and liqueur. Toss to mix well. Cover and refrigerate until needed.

Place almonds in a small skillet over medium-low heat. Toast nuts until they are lightly browned. Transfer to a zipper bag and set aside.

Place whipping cream in the bowl of an electric mixer and beat until frothy. Slowly add confectioners' sugar and almond extract, beating constantly until stiff peaks form. Transfer whipped cream to a covered container and refrigerate until needed.

To serve: Divide strawberries among 4 tulip-shaped wine glasses. Top with a generous dollop of whipped cream. Sprinkle toasted almonds atop whipped cream.

(SERVES 4)

Kayakers explore the rocky shores of Lake Superior.
BAYFIELD CHAMBER OF COMMERCE

Breakfast All Day

Apple Sausage Puffed Pancake

This puffy, baked, German-style pancake is commonly called a Dutch Baby. It deflates when you take it out of the oven. The pancake batter comes together in a mere five minutes. While the pancake bakes, you are free to prepare the savory topping.

2 tablespoons butter, divided

½ cup flour

½ cup milk

2 large eggs, beaten

3 tablespoons plus 2 teaspoons sugar, divided

½ teaspoon vanilla

Dash salt

3 to 4 ounces spicy pork sausage

1 cup chopped sweet onions, like Vidalia

2 large sweet-tart apples, like Fuji or Gala, cored, peeled, and cut into ½-inch dice

1 tablespoon confectioners' sugar

Preheat oven to 425 degrees F. Place 1 tablespoon butter in a 10-inch glass pie plate. Place pie plate on middle rack in oven to melt butter.

Whisk flour and milk together in a medium bowl. Add eggs, 3 tablespoons sugar, vanilla, and salt. Whisk to combine. Pour atop melted butter in pie plate. (Do not mix batter into butter.) Return plate to oven and bake 15 to 18 minutes, until pancake is puffed and golden.

While pancake is baking, cook sausage in a large nonstick skillet over medium heat until cooked through, stirring frequently to break sausage into bits, about 3 minutes. With a slotted spoon, remove sausage to paper toweling to drain. Add onions to skillet and sauté for 4 minutes, until soft and slightly browned. Remove to a small plate with a slotted spoon.

Melt remaining 1 tablespoon butter in skillet. Add apples and sprinkle with 2 teaspoons sugar. Sauté until softened but still crisp, about 2 minutes. Reduce heat to low. Return sausage and onions to skillet and stir to combine. Cook, stirring frequently, until mixture is heated through, about 2 minutes.

To serve: Cut puffed pancake into quarters. Transfer 1 wedge to each of 4 plates. Top each portion with one-quarter of the apple-sausage mixture. Sprinkle each portion with confectioners' sugar. Serve immediately.

(SERVES 4)

Bacon-Egg Rolls

I like to use Martin's Slider Potato rolls in this recipe, but any three-inch slider roll will suffice.

4 precut slider rolls

1 tablespoon butter, melted

¼ cup crispy, cooked, crumbled bacon

3 large eggs

1 teaspoon snipped fresh chives

1 teaspoon snipped fresh cilantro

1 teaspoon snipped fresh basil

1 teaspoon snipped fresh flat-leafed parsley

Salt and freshly ground black pepper

¼ cup shredded Swiss cheese

Preheat oven to 400 degrees F. Remove top from each roll and set aside. Using a small fork, pull the crumb from each roll, leaving a hollow shell. (If you accidentally break through the outside of the roll, press some crumb back into it.) Brush the inside of each roll with melted butter. Place 1 tablespoon crumbled bacon in the bottom of each roll.

Whisk eggs in a small bowl with herbs and salt and pepper to taste. Pour egg mixture evenly among the 4 hollow bread roll shells.

Place rolls on a baking sheet. Bake for 15 minutes or until eggs are nearly set. Mound 1 tablespoon cheese atop each egg roll. Place roll tops on baking sheet. Bake cheese-topped rolls and tops for 5 minutes. Place tops on egg rolls and serve immediately.

(SERVES 4)

Eggnog French Toast

Legend has it that French toast dates back to ancient Rome, where the Romans dipped bread in milk and eggs and then fried it. This eggnog version may become a Christmas classic.

2 cups commercially prepared eggnog

2 large eggs

¼ teaspoon cinnamon

⅛ teaspoon nutmeg

1 loaf (16 ounces) cinnamon swirl bread

1 tablespoon butter or margarine

2 tablespoons confectioners' sugar

Fresh fruit, for serving

Whisk eggnog, eggs, cinnamon, and nutmeg together in a medium bowl. Place 8 slices of bread in a 10 x 13-inch baking dish. Place 4 slices of bread in an 8 x 8-inch baking dish. Pour eggnog mixture over bread in both dishes, so that bread is totally covered and soaks in the liquid.

Place 3 large nonstick skillets or griddle pans over medium heat. Grease each pan with butter. Add soaked bread slices to skillets. Cook bread for 2 minutes or until underside is golden. Turn each with a firm spatula. Cook for 1 to 2 minutes more, until undersides are golden. Place confectioners' sugar in a small strainer and sprinkle over French toast. Serve immediately with a side of fresh fruit.

(SERVES 6, 2 SLICES PER PERSON)

Faux Crab Freezer Quiche

If you're lucky enough to have a cabin Up North, you know that family and friends descend upon you frequently, all summer long. This is a great go-to breakfast to serve when that happens, because, made ahead and frozen, the quiche goes straight from freezer to the oven. No fuss, no mess, no work! Get creative and experiment with different combinations of ingredients and make a freezer full of quiches that will last you until the leaves start to turn.

5 large eggs

½ cup heavy cream

¼ cup milk

¾ teaspoon salt

¼ teaspoon garlic powder

½ cup shredded Swiss cheese

½ cup shredded cheddar cheese

1 (8-ounce) package imitation crabmeat, flaked (pollock)

1 tablespoon fresh snipped dill

1 premade frozen deep-dish pie crust

Whisk together all ingredients except pie crust until well combined. Pour mixture into pie crust. Carefully transfer filled pie crust, uncovered, to freezer. (Make sure it can lie flat.) When quiche is frozen, wrap it in foil, label, and return it to the freezer.

When ready to use, preheat oven to 375 degrees F. Do not thaw quiche. Place frozen quiche on a cookie sheet. Remove wrapping and then loosely cover quiche with aluminum foil. Bake for 50 minutes. Remove foil and bake 20 to 30 minutes more or until golden.

Chef's note: You can use just about any combination of ingredients in this recipe. Try it with 4 ounces chopped prosciutto or ham, 4 ounces chiffonade-cut fresh spinach, and a fresh herb of your choice. The hardest part of the recipe is to transfer the liquid quiche to the freezer!

(SERVES 4)

Juustoleipä

Juustoleipä (pronounced *YOO-stoh-LAY-pah*) is a buttery-flavored, flat, squeaky cheese made in Finland for more than 200 years. It made its way to northern Wisconsin with Scandinavian immigrants, centuries ago. Juustoleipä, which literally means "cheese bread" in Finnish, is sold as a flat rectangle or square with a splotchy brown crust. After the juustoleipä curds (which are similar in texture to feta) are pressed into blocks, they are baked in a special oven, whose heat caramelizes the sugars on the outside of the cheese. "It may be the only cheese in the world to be baked during the cheese-making process," says cheese expert James Path from the Wisconsin Center for dairy research.

Warmed in a skillet until it glistens, juusto, as it is often called, does not melt and has a mild, buttery flavor. It looks like French toast but tastes like a grilled cheese sandwich without the bread. Cut into strips, juusto is often eaten for breakfast or dessert with jam, honey, or syrup. Laplanders in Finland used to dunk it in their breakfast coffee!

Legend has it that Finnish mothers of eligible, unmarried daughters would offer juusto to potential suitors and if the man liked the cheese, he got the option to marry the girl. Legend also claims that juustoleipä was originally made from reindeer milk in Finland. Today, both in Europe and in Wisconsin, juustoleipä is made from pasteurized cow's milk.

About a half-dozen cheesemakers in Wisconsin make juustoleipä, often labelled as juusto, bread cheese, or baked cheese. You can find it online at pasturepridecheese.com.

Juusto Coulis

Coulis is a thick sauce made with pureed fruit. It will keep in the refrigerator for up to one week and can be frozen for up to one month.

3 cups (1 pound) sliced fresh strawberries

6 tablespoons plus 1 teaspoon confectioners' sugar

2 tablespoons peach schnapps

2 (6-ounce) blocks juustoleipä

To make the strawberry coulis: Place strawberries and 2 tablespoons confectioners' sugar in a blender. Pulse until strawberries are roughly pureed. Add remaining confectioners' sugar and pulse to combine. Add schnapps and blend until smooth. Transfer to plastic squeeze bottles. (Makes 2½ cups.)

Warm juustoleipä in a large nonstick skillet over medium heat for 2 to 3 minutes per side. Transfer cheese to a cutting board and cut it into 1-inch strips. Drizzle each strip with strawberry coulis. Transfer to a serving tray and serve warm.

(SERVES 4 TO 6)

Ham-Artichoke-Tomato Frittata

A frittata is actually an Italian omelet loaded with an assortment of savory ingredients. It is not folded over, like a traditional French omelet, but instead cooked slowly on the stove, then finished in the oven. Versatile in every way, frittatas are great for breakfast, brunch, lunch, or supper, and can be eaten hot, at room temperature, or even cold.

1 tablespoon canola oil

½ cup diced ham

¼ cup chopped sweet onions, like Vidalia

½ cup chopped artichoke hearts

¼ cup sliced grape tomatoes

6 large eggs, beaten

½ cup shredded mild cheddar cheese

2 tablespoons finely snipped fresh basil or 2 teaspoons dried

Sour cream, salsa, Parmesan cheese, or baby greens, for serving

Preheat oven to 350 degrees F. Heat oil in a 10-inch nonstick, ovenproof skillet over medium heat. Add ham and onions and sauté for 30 seconds, stirring constantly. Add artichoke hearts and tomatoes and cook for 30 seconds more, stirring constantly. Reduce heat to low. Pour beaten eggs evenly over filling ingredients. Sprinkle cheese and basil atop egg mixture.

Slowly cook frittata for about 13 minutes, or until the eggs have firmed up around the perimeter and only the center is still slightly runny. Transfer skillet to oven and bake until center has just set, 3 to 5 minutes more. (Eggs will continue to set up when frittata is removed from the oven.)

Using a firm spatula, transfer frittata to a large cutting board. Cut frittata into thirds. Serve the frittata topped with a dollop of sour cream or salsa, a sprinkle of freshly grated Parmesan cheese, or place frittata on a bed of baby greens dressed with your favorite vinaigrette.

Chef's note: When filling a frittata, ingredient possibilities are limited only by your imagination. Follow the simple formula in the recipe above and you can design your own creation. For a 10-inch frittata that generously serves 3, heartily serves 2, or conservatively serves 4, you'll need 1 tablespoon oil, 6 large eggs, 2 cups filling ingredients (in total), and 2 tablespoons freshly snipped herbs or 2 teaspoons dried herbs. Be sure to prepare all your ingredients before you start cooking the frittata. It goes together very quickly.

(SERVES 3)

Loaded Oatmeal

We all know that the best part of oatmeal is all the "stuff" we put on top of it. This master recipe loads the oatmeal with nuts and dried fruits. Use it to make Stovetop Oatmeal or try the Baked Oatmeal creation below.

Master Recipe

4 cups Quaker Old-Fashioned oats (not quick-cooking oats)

¼ cup chopped walnuts

½ cup sliced almonds

¼ cup roasted sunflower seeds

¼ cup dried cherries

¼ cup dried cranberries

¼ cup chopped dates

¼ cup chopped dried apricots

1 teaspoon cinnamon

Mix all ingredients together in a large bowl. Transfer to an airtight covered container and keep in pantry until needed, up to 3 months.

(MAKES 6 CUPS)

Stovetop Oatmeal

In Scotland, oatmeal is served in one bowl, milk in another. Diners dip each spoonful of hot oatmeal in the cold milk, therefore keeping the milk from cooling off the oatmeal.

1¼ cups oatmeal mix

Milk or half-and-half

Brown sugar

Place 2 cups water in a medium saucepan over high heat. When water has come to a boil, add 1¼ cups oatmeal mix. Reduce heat to low and cook, uncovered, stirring occasionally, 12 minutes, until water is absorbed. Cover and allow oatmeal to rest for 2 minutes. Serve oatmeal with milk or half-and-half. Sprinkle with brown sugar to taste.

(SERVES 3 TO 4)

Baked Oatmeal

1⅓ cups oatmeal mix

½ cup milk

½ cup apple juice

¼ cup brown sugar

1 teaspoon vanilla

1 large egg, beaten

1 teaspoon baking powder

Milk or half-and-half, for serving

Preheat oven to 350 degrees F. Coat a pie plate with vegetable cooking spray.

In a large bowl, combine oatmeal mix, milk, juice, brown sugar, vanilla, egg, and baking powder and stir to mix well. Pour mixture into prepared pie plate. Bake for 20 to 25 minutes, until oatmeal is almost set. Remove from oven and allow oatmeal to rest for 5 minutes. Serve each portion with milk or half-and-half.

(SERVES 4 TO 6)

Monkey Breads

This sweet pull-apart breakfast cake, also known as bubble loaf, became popular in the 1950s and reached star status when Nancy Reagan served it at the White House in the 1980s. Actually, the bread is a descendant of the sweet, buttery, cinnamon yeast rolls first made in ancient times by Middle Eastern cooks. Recipes and spices traveled to Europe with crusaders, traders, and explorers, eventually reaching the New World. The technique of combining tiny balls of prepared dough in one pan was popular in the United States as far back as the mid-nineteenth century, when pioneers and cowboys made one-pot baked goods in portable Dutch ovens over open campfires. Lots of far-fetched theories about the origin of the name monkey bread *have abounded over the years. Most probable? The balled bread resembles the gourd-shaped fruit of the African baobab tree—much favored by monkeys—which is called monkey bread.*

Caramel Monkey Bread

½ cup butter, divided

⅓ cup chopped pecans or walnuts or a mixture of the two, divided

1 cup firmly packed brown sugar

½ teaspoon cinnamon

½ cup orange marmalade

2 (12-ounce) packages refrigerated flaky biscuits, such as Pillsbury Golden Layers

Preheat oven to 375°F. In small saucepan over medium-low heat, melt butter. Place two tablespoons melted butter into a Bundt pan. With a basting brush, coat bottom and sides of pan with the butter. Sprinkle 3 tablespoons chopped nuts over bottom of prepared pan.

Place remaining nuts, brown sugar, cinnamon, and marmalade in the saucepan with the remaining butter. Stir to combine ingredients. Heat to boiling, stirring occasionally. Remove pan from heat and set aside.

Meanwhile, separate dough into biscuits. Cut each biscuit in half and roll each into a ball. Place balls from first can of biscuits (24) in bottom of prepared Bundt pan. Drizzle half of the caramel sauce over balls. Repeat with another layer of dough balls, topped with remaining caramel sauce. Bake for 20 to 25 minutes or until browned and slightly crusty. Invert immediately onto serving platter and remove pan. Allow cake to cool for 10 minutes before serving.

(SERVES 8)

Orange Monkey Bread

⅓ cup butter, melted, plus 1 tablespoon hard butter

1 cup sugar

Grated zest from 1 orange

3 tablespoons freshly squeezed orange juice

1 (24-roll) package frozen Parker House–style dough rolls

The night before: Generously butter a 9 x 13-inch baking dish with 1 tablespoon hard butter. Mix sugar, melted butter, orange zest, and orange juice together in a small bowl. Pour into buttered pan. Place dough rolls atop orange mixture.

Coat a sheet of waxed paper with vegetable cooking spray. Place atop rolls in baking dish. Place dish on kitchen counter overnight.

In the morning: Preheat oven to 350 degrees F. Discard waxed paper. Bake monkey bread for 20 to 25 minutes. Remove monkey bread from oven and flip over onto serving platter. Drizzle any remaining orange mixture over the monkey bread. Serve immediately.

Chef's note: Parker House rolls are buttery yeast rolls named after Boston's Parker House Hotel where they first were made in the 1870s. Substitute Rhodes Frozen Rolls (15-count) or Mary B's Tea Biscuits (24-count), or any other brand comparable frozen rolls from your supermarket if can't find the Parker House–style rolls.

(SERVES 8 TO 10)

Danish Kringle

We have Danish immigrant bakers to thank for the creation of Wisconsin's remarkable state pastry—the kringle—the recipe and baking expertise of which they brought to Racine in the 1800s.

Kringle (pronounced *KRING-gul*) is a flat oval pastry made with thirty-six layers of flaky, buttery dough and a variety of fruit, nut, or gourmet fillings. It measures approximately 14 x 12 inches and weighs about a pound and a half. The soul of the pastry is its flaky dough, which is hand-folded over and over, creating eighteen layers. The dough rests for three days. Once ready, it is hand-wrapped around the filling, then hand-shaped into a large oval. The kringles are baked to a golden brown and then hand-drizzled with icing.

Still made using traditional methods in Racine today by several bakeries, kringle is widely available all over Wisconsin. Once tasted, it is quite impossible to settle for any other Danish-style pastry. Racine Danish Kringles has been family owned and operated for three generations. O&H Danish Bakery has been operated by the Olesen family for sixty-five years, and Bendtsen's Bakery has been in business since 1934. (All ship their kringles nationwide.)

Kringle was named Wisconsin's official state pastry on June 30, 2013.

RACINE DANISH KRINGLES

Potato Pancakes

I can still see my grandma peeling potatoes and onions at our Wisconsin cabin, while my grandpa sat at the table grating them all by hand into a big bowl. Grandma made her breakfast potato pancakes one at a time, the size of the skillet. We all were required to be on deck when it came our turn to eat. You can bet we stood in line!

2 very large or 4 small Yukon Gold potatoes

½ large sweet onion, like Vidalia

1 large egg

1 teaspoon salt

2 tablespoons flour

4 tablespoons butter, divided

Butter, applesauce, or sour cream, for serving

Preheat oven to 250 degrees F. Place a nonstick baking sheet on middle rack.

Grate potatoes and onion into the bowl of a food processor. Place grated mixture in a strainer and press on potatoes with the back of a spoon to drain excess liquid. Place chopping blade in processor, then add grated potatoes and onion, egg, salt, and flour. Pulse just until mixture is combined. Transfer mixture to a medium bowl.

Melt 2 tablespoons butter in a large nonstick skillet over medium heat. Add 3 half-cup measures of

potato mixture to skillet, placing well apart. Flatten mixture with a firm spatula. Cook potato pancakes for 3 minutes, until browned on the underside. Then flip pancakes and cook 2 minutes more. Transfer pancakes to baking sheet in oven to keep them warm while you cook the second batch of pancakes.

Repeat process with remaining potato pancake batter. Serve immediately with butter, applesauce, and/or sour cream.

Chef's note: For truly authentic German-style Wisconsin potato pancakes à la Grandma, grate the potatoes and the onions using a box grater.

(MAKES 6 DESSERT-PLATE-SIZE PANCAKES)

On-the-Go Sausage Quiches

Family-owned and -operated since 1945, Wisconsin's Johnsonville sausages are the most popular sausage brand in the United States and are available in more than forty-five countries.

4 ounces Johnsonville uncooked maple pork sausage

½ cup chopped sweet onions, like Vidalia

½ cup chopped roasted red peppers (from a jar)

6 large eggs

½ cup heavy whipping cream

½ teaspoon hot sauce

1 (12-ounce) package Pillsbury Golden Layers Honey Butter biscuits

1½ cups shredded mild cheddar cheese

Preheat oven to 400 degrees F. Brown sausage and onions in a medium nonstick skillet over medium heat, about 3 minutes, stirring and breaking up the sausage into bite-size pieces. Remove from heat and stir in red peppers. In a medium bowl, beat eggs with a wire whisk. Whisk in whipping cream and hot sauce.

Coat a 12-count cupcake pan with vegetable cooking spray. Divide each of 6 biscuits in half, horizontally, and place one in the bottom of each cup. (Press dough so that it completely covers the bottom.)

Divide 1 cup cheese among the 12 cups. Divide sausage mixture among the cups and place atop

cheese. Pour egg batter equally among the cups (about 2 ounces per), Sprinkle remaining cheese atop egg mixture.

Bake for 10 to 12 minutes, until eggs are set and a wooden skewer inserted in the center of one quiche comes out clean. Remove pan from oven and run a small, firm, plastic spatula around edges of each quiche. Then gently place tip of spatula under each quiche and remove it from the muffin cup. Serve one quiche per person for a light breakfast, two for a hearty breakfast.

(MAKES 12 MINIATURE QUICHES)

Index

"The Gang's All Here" Salad, 143
All Berry Sauce, 193
Apple-Sausage Puffed Pancake, 200
Apricot Baked Brie, 2
Aunt Rita's Tried-and-True Two-Bean Chili, 26
Babycakes, 174
Bacon-Egg Rolls, 201
Baked Goat Cheese Stuffed Tomatoes, 148
Baked Nachos, 3
Banana Banshee, 195
Barbecued Jumbo Shrimp, 129
Beer Can Chicken, 110
Beer Cheese Dips, 10
Beer-Marinated Sirloin Steak, 91
Blackberry-Glazed Pork Tenderloin, 103
"BLT" Soup, 27
Blue Cheese Dressing, 136
Blue Tail Fly, 195
Braciole, 68
Brandy Old Fashioned, 22
Brown Sugar Beer Sausage, 4
Brown Sugar Pork Loin Roast, 102
Butter Burger Sliders, 50
Butternut Squash–Pear Soup, 28
Butterscotch Sauce, 193
Call of the Loon, 16
Candied Carrots, 149
Cheesy Baked Hash Browns, 156
Cherry-Fudge Babycakes, 175
Chicken Pot Pies, 78
Classic Carrot Babycakes, 174
Cocktail Skewers, 5
Company Meatloaf with Cranberry
   Ketchup, 94
Cookout Kabobs, 112
Cottage Pies, 80
Cranberry Ketchup, 99
Cranberry Wild Rice, 162
Death by Chocolate Mousse Trifle, 176
Dirty Rice Pilaf, 168
Drunken Strawberries with Almond Whipped
   Cream, 196
Eggnog French Toast, 202
Emmentaler Cheese Bread, 171
Endive and Pear Salad with Champagne
   Vinaigrette, 137
English Trifle, 177
Family Heirloom Christmas Sugar
   Cookies, 187

Faux Crab Freezer Quiche, 203
Faux Seafood Biscuit Baskets, 8
Fish and Chips, 119
Four-Cheese Macaroni and Cheese, 74
French Onion Soup, 31
Fried Cheese Curds, 6
German Potato Salad, 158
Gingered Carrot Vichyssoise, 34
Greek Meatballs, 61
Greek Meatballs with Mediterranean-Sauced
   Penne, 63
Grilled Bruschetta Walleye Fillets, 120
Grilled Five-Cheese Sandwiches, 48
Grilled Marinated Swordfish, 121
Grilled Rack of Lamb, 109
Grill-Roasted Turkey with Orange-Molasses
   Glaze, 115
Ham-Artichoke-Tomato Frittata, 206
Hamburger Stroganoff, 69
Hawaiian Meatballs, 61
Hawaiian Meatballs in Sweet and Sour Sauce
   with Coconut Orzo, 65
Hodag Brisket, 107
Hoisin–Ale Braised Short Ribs, 95
Honey-Mustard Vinaigrette, 135
Hot Apple Slaw, 138
Hot Fudge Sauce, 192
Hot Mulled Cider, 20
Hot Super Sub, 47
Italian Meatless Sauce, 67
Juusto Coulis, 204
Korean Short Rib Bulgogi Tacos with Creamy
   Lime Vinaigrette, 53
Lake Trout Piccata, 122
Lemon-Sauced Crab Cakes, 130
Lemon–Poppy Seed Dressing, 136
Loaded Oatmeal, 207
Lumberjack Baked Beans, 167
Make-Ahead Fresh Peach Pie, 182
Mango Tango Summer Cooler, 14
Maple Bacon Crack, 180
Meatball Base, 60
Mercer Moonshine, 16
Mexican Burrito Pie, 85
Monkey Breads, 209
Mushroom Pastry Pinwheels, 9
Mushroom Soup, 35
Mustard and Jack Daniel's Marinated Sirloin
   Steak, 90

On-the-Go Sausage Quiches, 215
Orange Shrimp Stir Fry over Jasmine
  Rice, 128
Orange-Mustard Glazed Baked Ham with
  Horseradish Cream Sauce, 104
Parmesan Risotto with Ham, Baby Spinach,
  and Slivered Tomatoes, 169
Pasta e Fagioli, 38
Peartini Irene, 14
Pizza Pot Pie, 87
Plum-Ginger Chicken Wings, 114
Pork and Apple Pie, 86
Potato Pancakes, 213
Pumpkin Satin Cheesecake Pie, 186
Rainbow Summer Tomato Salad, 139
Raspberry Vinaigrette, 135
Ravioli Lasagna, 72
Red Currant Glazed Corned Beef with
  Horseradish Cream, 96
Roast Duck with Fruited Orange Sauce, 116
Roasted Butternut Squash and Sweet
  Potato–Pesto Mash, 150
Salmon in Puff Pastry, 123
Salt and Vinegar Baby Red Potatoes, 157
Sangria, 15
Sauerbraten, 100
Shredded Pork and Sauerkraut Sammies, 52
Sicilian Meatballs, 61

Sicilian Meatballs in Fresh Tomato Sauce with
  Spaghetti, 66
Slow Cooker Booyah, 37
Smoked Salmon Egg Salad, 54
Smothered Cube Steaks, 97
Spaghetti Squash Primavera, 153
Spicy Minted Thai-Marinated Grilled Pork
  Chops, 108
Spinach Salad with Warm Bacon
  Dressing, 142
Split Pea Soup, 40
Stir Fry Your Way, 126
Summertime Lemonade, 21
Thai Meatballs, 61
Thai Meatballs in Red Curry Orzo, 64
Three Sisters Salad, 141
Tom and Jerry Cocktail, 19
Twice-Baked Stuffed Potatoes, 164
Up North Loaded Bloody Mary, 13
Up North Pasties, 45
Upside-Down Dill-Salmon Loaf Pie with
  Lemon Sauce, 82
Vegan Chocolate Peppermint Crinkle
  Cookies, 190
Versatile Vegetables: Four Sauces, 144
Wava's Family Favorite Pot Roast, 101
Wava's Foolproof Scalloped Potatoes, 163
Wisconsin Beer Cheese Soup, 41
Wisconsin-Style Beer Bratwurst, 57

Acknowledgments

Back in the 1960s, the Beatles sang, "I get by with a little help from my friends," and that lyric has rung true for every book project I have undertaken for the past twenty-eight years. Way back in the 1950s, comedian Bob Hope each week ended his television show with the tune, "Thanks for the Memories," which also rings true for the *Way Up North Wisconsin Cookbook*. Had my mother and father not found their little piece of God's country Way Up North while on their honeymoon in the 1940s, this cookbook would not exist. So, thanks for the memories, Mom and Dad.

Thank you also to my fearless taste testers—my husband, Bob; my children and grandchildren; and my wonderful friends (you know who you are), who all love to share our special place each summer.

A special thank-you to Bayfield and Rhinelander Chambers of Commerce, Dairy Farmers of Wisconsin, CT's Deli, and Racine Danish Kringles for providing requested photography. And thanks to Midwest Maple and Wava and Katelyn Hawker for their recipe submissions and accompanying images.

Finally, my gratitude to Amy Lyons, Kristan Schiller, and all the great folks at Globe Pequot, for allowing me to bring *Way Up North* to life.

About the Author

A University of Wisconsin graduate, **Victoria Shearer** wore several professional hats—elementary school teacher, advertising agency account executive, cooking magazine copy editor—before combining her passion for food and travel with her love of writing. For the past twenty-nine years, she has written for many national magazines and newspapers and is author of ten editions of *Insiders' Guide to the Florida Keys & Key West*, as well as *Walking Places in New England*, *It Happened in the Florida Keys*, and *The Florida Keys Cookbook*.

Vicki and her husband, Bob, divide their time between Wake Forest, North Carolina, and their cabin Way Up North in Mercer, Wisconsin. No day is complete without puttering in the kitchen, but she also loves to play mah jongg, do needlepoint, and cheer on her beloved Carolina Hurricanes hockey team. And while the titles of "author" and "cook" are quite nice, Vicki's most cherished monikers are "Mom" (Brian, Kristen, and John) and "Grammy" (Christopher, Dona, Bethany, Bobby, Ashleigh, Leia, Nicholas, and Sammy).